Successfully Utilizing CMMS/EAM Systems

Terry Wireman, CPMM
www.terrywireman.com
TLWireman@Mindspring.com

Maintenance Strategy Series

Volume 4
Successfully Utilizing CMMS/EAM Systems
Terry Wireman

ISBN 978-0-9832258-7-4
HF062020

First Edition, 2009

Publisher: Reliabilityweb.com

For information: Reliabilityweb.com
www.reliabilityweb.com
8991 Daniels Center Drive, Suite 105, Ft. Myers, FL 33912
Toll Free: 888-575-1245 | Phone: 239-333-2500
E-mail: crm@reliabilityweb.com

20   19   18   17   16   15

TABLE OF CONTENTS

Introduction

Volume 4 CMMS / EAM Systems

In this volume, the topic of a computerized maintenance management system (CMMS) is discussed. In the first volumes of the Maintenance Strategy Series, almost all of the documentation necessary to management maintenance can be handled manually. However, with the addition of the maintenance work management processes in the last volume (Volume 3 of the Maintenance Strategy Series), the documentation and data analysis necessary to be efficient has increased.

It is still possible for some maintenance departments to manage their information manually. However, it is more efficient to use a properly-designed computer system to accomplish these tasks. Continuing with manual systems would be analogous to a company's accounting department still trying to utilize pens and lined ledger paper to track the company financials. Given the current stage of computer technology, it is much more logical to use a computer system to track and manage the necessary business information to manage maintenance properly.

A computerized maintenance management system is designed to simplify the data collection and analysis. As will be explained in this text, the basic modules of the CMMS are designed to facilitate the management of the various components of maintenance, such as:
- Preventive maintenance
- MRO inventory and procurement
- Work order management, including the tracking of
- Labor costs and information
- Material cost and information
- Contracting cost and information

When the CMMS is utilized across multiple plants, and corporate managers use the data to manage the assets at an enterprise level, the system acronym changes to an EAM system or Enterprise Asset Management system. This text will help the reader differentiate between the two types of systems and provide guidelines on when to use each type of system.

The text contains valuable information that will help any one using a CMMS / EAM system, whether they are in the selection, implementation, or utilization phase with their system.

Overview

The Maintenance Strategy Series Process Flow

Good, sound, functional maintenance practices are essential for effective maintenance / asset management strategies. But what exactly are "good, sound, functional maintenance practices?" The materials contained in this overview (and the overview for each of the volumes in the Maintenance Strategy Series) explain each block of the Maintenance Strategy Series Process Flow. They are designed to highlight the steps necessary to develop a complete maintenance / asset management strategy for your plant or facility. The activities described in the Process Flow are designed to serve as a guide for strategic planning discussions. The flow diagram for the Maintenance Strategy Series Process Flow can be found at the end of this overview.

Author's Note

Many individuals may believe that this type of maintenance strategy program is too expensive or time consuming to implement, especially when there are advanced predictive or reliability techniques that might be employed. Yet there is a reason for the sequencing of the Maintenance Strategy Series process flow. If attempts are made to deploy advanced techniques before the organization is mature enough to properly understand and utilize them (basically, the "I want results now" short-term focus), they will fail. The reason? Developing and implementing a sustainable maintenance / asset management strategy is more than just distributing a flow chart or dictionary of technical terms. It is an educational exercise that must change a company culture. The educational process that occurs during a structured implementation of basic maintenance processes must evolve into more sophisticated and advanced processes as the organization develops the understanding and skills necessary.

If an individual is to obtain a college degree, it may involve an investment of four or more years to achieve this goal. Likewise, if a company is to obtain an advanced standing in a maintenance / asset management strategy, it may take up to four years. It is not that someone cannot,

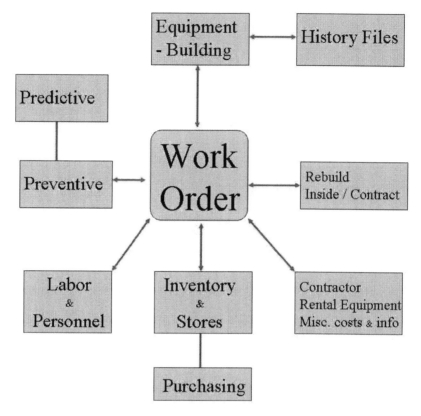

Figure I-4 Work Order and MRO Cost Relationships

through years of experience and education, design their maintenance / asset management process in a short time period. It will, however, take the entire organization (from senior executive to shop floor employees) this amount of time to become mature in their understanding and utilization of the process. Although there will be incremental benefits achieved along the journey to maintenance / asset management excellence, the true benefits are not realized until there is a complete organizational focus on maximizing all aspects of the investment in the assets. It is this competitive focus that separates long-term, sustainable success from a short-term "flash" of improvement.

In the beginning, it is necessary for a plant or facility to decide it is necessary to improve their maintenance / asset management strategy. The business reason for the needed improvement can be multi-faceted, but would likely include:

- Poor Return On Investment (ROI) for the total plant or facility valuation
- Poor throughput for the design of the plant
- Inability to meet production demands
- High cost of occupancy for a facility
- Excessive downtime
- Production inefficiencies

Once the decision has been made to develop / improve the maintenance/ asset management strategy, the Maintenance Strategy Series process flow diagram should be followed. It begins with Preventive Maintenance.

1. Does a PM Program Exist?

Preventive maintenance is the core of any equipment/asset maintenance process improvement strategy. All plant and facility equipment, including special back-up or redundant equipment, must be covered by a complete, cost-effective, preventive maintenance program. The preventive maintenance program must be designed to eliminate all unplanned equipment failures. The preventive maintenance program should be designed to insure proper coverage of the critical equipment of the plant or facility. The

MRO Inventory Best Practices

- 95 - 97% Service Levels
- 100% accuracy of data
- > 1 turn per year on inventory value
- Elimination of non-moving spares
- Reduction of slow moving spares
- Controlled access
- Consignment arrangements
- Strategic partnering with suppliers

Figure I-5 MRO Inventory Best Practices

program should include a good cross section of the following:
- Inspections
- Adjustments
- Lubrication
- Proactive replacements of worn components

The goal of the program is to insure there will be no unplanned equipment downtime.

2. Is the PM Program Effective?

The effectiveness of the preventive maintenance program is determined by the level of unplanned equipment maintenance that is performed. Unplanned equipment maintenance is defined as any maintenance activity that is performed with less than one week of advanced planning. Unplanned equipment maintenance is commonly referred to as reactive maintenance. An effective preventive maintenance program will reduce the amount of unplanned work to less than 20% of the total manpower expended for all equipment maintenance activities. If more time than this is being spent on unplanned activities, then a reevaluation of the preventive maintenance program is required. It will take more resources and additional time to make progress in any of the following maintenance process areas unless the preventive maintenance program is effective enough for the equipment maintenance to meet the 80%/20% rule.

It should be the goal of not progressing any further until the preventive maintenance program is successful. In addition to requiring more resources and taking longer to develop the subsequent maintenance processes, it is very common to see companies try to compensate for a reactive organization. This means they will circumvent some of the "best practices' in the subsequent processes to make them work in a reactive environment. All this will do is reinforce negative behavior and sub-optimize the effectiveness of the subsequent processes.

3. Do MRO Processes Exist?

After the preventive maintenance program is effective, the equipment spares, stores, and purchasing systems must be analyzed. The equipment spares and stores should be organized, with all of the spares identified and tagged, stored in an identified location, with accurate on-hand and usage data. The purchasing system must allow for procurement of all necessary spare parts to meet the maintenance schedules. All data necessary to track the cost and usage of all spare parts must be complete and accurate.

4. Are the MRO Processes Effective?

The benchmark for an effective maintenance / asset management MRO process is service level. Simply defined, the service level measures what percent of the time a part is in stock when it is needed. The spare parts must be on hand at least 95%– 97% of the time for the stores and purchasing systems to support the maintenance planning and scheduling functions.

Again, unless maintenance activities are proactive (less than 20% unplanned weekly), it will be impossible for the stores and purchasing groups to be cost effective in meeting equipment maintenance spare parts demands. They will either fall below the 95%–97% service level, or they will be forced to carry excess inventory to meet the desired service level.

The MRO process must be effective for the next steps in the strategy development. If the MRO data required to support the maintenance work management process is not developed, the maintenance spare parts costs will never be accurate to an equipment level. The need for this level of data accuracy will be explained in Sections 6 and 10 of the preface.

5. Does a Work Management Process Exist?

The work management system is designed to track all equipment maintenance activities. The activities can be anything from inspections and adjustments to major overhauls. Any maintenance that is performed without being recorded in the work order system is lost. Lost or unrecorded data makes it impossible to perform any analysis of equipment problems. All activities performed on equipment must be recorded to a work order by the responsible individual. This highlights the point that maintenance, operations, and engineering will be extremely involved in utilizing work orders.

Beyond just having a work order, the process of using a work order system needs detailed. A comprehensive work management process should include details on the following:

- How to request work
- How to prioritize work
- How to plan work
- How to schedule work
- How to execute work

- How to record work details
- How to process follow up work
- How to analyze historical work details

6. Is the Work Management Process Effective?

This question should be answered by performing an evaluation of the equipment maintenance data. The evaluation may be as simple as answering the following questions:

- How complete is the data?
- How accurate is the data?
- How timely is the data?
- How usable is the data?

If the data is not complete, it will be impossible to perform any meaningful analysis of the equipment historical and current condition. If the data is not accurate, it will be impossible to correctly identify the root cause of any equipment problems. If the data is not timely, then it will be impossible to correct equipment problems before they cause equipment failures. If the data is not usable, it will be impossible to format it in a manner that allows for any meaningful analysis. Unless the work order system provides data that passes this evaluation, it is impossible to make further progress.

7. Is Planning and Scheduling Utilized?

This review examines the policies and practices for equipment maintenance planning and scheduling. Although this is a subset of the work management process, it needs a separate evaluation. The goal of planning and scheduling is to optimize any resources expended on equipment maintenance activities, while minimizing the interruption the activities have on the production schedule. A common term used in many organizations is "wrench time." This refers to the time the craft technicians have their hands on tools and are actually performing work; as opposed to being delayed or waiting to work. The average reactive organization may have a wrench time of only 20%, whereas a proactive, planned, and scheduled organization may be as high as 60% or even a little more.

The ultimate goal of planning and scheduling is to insure that all equipment maintenance activities occur like a pit stop in a NASCAR race. This insures optimum equipment uptime, with quality equipment maintenance activities being performed. Planning and scheduling pulls together all of the activities, (maintenance, operations, and engineering) and focuses them on obtaining maximum (quality) results in a minimum amount of time.

8. Is Planning and Scheduling Effective?

Although this question is similar to #6, the focus is on the efficiency and effectiveness of the activities performed in the 80% planned mode. An efficient planning and scheduling program will insure maximum productivity of the employees performing any equipment maintenance activities. Delays, such as waiting on or looking for parts, waiting on or looking for rental equipment, waiting on or looking for the equipment to be shut down, waiting on or looking for drawings, waiting on or looking for tools, will all be eliminated.

If these delays are not eliminated through planning and scheduling, then it will be impossible to optimize equipment utilization. It will be the same as a NASCAR pit crew taking too long to do a pit stop; the race is lost by not keeping the car on the track. The equipment utilization is lost by not properly keeping the equipment in service.

9. Is a CMMS / EAM System Utilized?

By this point in the Maintenance Strategy Process development, a considerable volume of data is being generated and tracked. Ultimately, the data becomes difficult to manage using manual methods. It may be necessary to computerize the work order system. If the workforce is burdened with excessive paper work and is accumulating file cabinets of equipment data that no one has time to look at, it is best to computerize the maintenance / asset management system. The systems that are used for managing the maintenance /asset management process are commonly referred to by acronyms such as CMMS (Computerized Maintenance Management Systems) or EAM (Enterprise Asset Management) systems. (The difference between the two types of systems will be thoroughly covered in Volume Four.)

The CMMS/ EAM System should be meeting the equipment management information requirements of the organization. Some of the requirements include:
- Complete tracking of all repairs and service
- The ability to develop reports, for example:
- Top ten equipment problems

- Most costly equipment to maintain
- Percent reactive vs. proactive maintenance
- Cost tracking of all parts and costs

If the CMMS/EAM system does not produce this level of data, then it needs to be re-evaluated and a new one may need to be implemented.

10. Is the CMMS/ EAM System Utilization Effective?

The re-evaluation of the CMMS / EAM system may also highlight areas of weakness in the utilization of the system. This should allow for the specification of new work management process steps that will correct the problems and allow for good equipment data to be collected. Several questions for consideration include:

- Is the data we are collecting complete and accurate?
- Is the data collection effort burdening the work force?
- Do we need to change the methods we use to manage the data?

Once problems are corrected and the CMMS / EAM system is being properly utilized, then constant monitoring for problems and solutions must be put into effect.

The CMMS / EAM system is a computerized version of a manual system. There are currently over 200 commercially produced CMMS / EAM systems in the North American market. Finding the correct one may take some time, but through the use of lists, surveys, and "word of mouth," it should take no more than three to a maximum of six months for any organization to select their CMMS / EAM system. When the right CMMS / EAM system is selected, it then must be implemented. CMMS / EAM system implementation may take from three months (smaller organizations) to as long as 18 months (large organizations) to implement. Companies can spend much time and energy around the issue of CMMS selection and implementation. It must be remembered that the CMMS / EAM system is only a tool to be used in the improvement process; it is not the goal of the process. Losing sight of this fact can curtail the effectiveness of any organization's path to continuous improvement.

If the correct CMMS / EAM system is being utilized, then it makes the equipment data collection faster and easier. It should also make the analysis of the data faster and easier. The CMMS / EAM system should assist in enforcing "World Class" maintenance disciplines, such as planning and scheduling and effective stores controls. The CMMS / EAM system should provide the employees with usable data with which to make

equipment management decisions. If the CMMS / EAM system is not improving these efforts, then the effective usage of the CMMS / EAM system needs to be evaluated. Some of the problems encountered with CMMS / EAM systems include:
- Failure to fully implement the CMMS
- Incomplete utilization of the CMMS
- Inaccurate data input into the CMMS
- Failure to use the data once it is in the CMMS

11. Do Maintenance Skills Training Programs Exist?

This question examines the maintenance skills training initiatives in the company. This is a critical item for any future steps because the maintenance organization is typically charged with providing training for any operations personnel that will be involved in future activities. Companies need to have an ongoing maintenance skills training program because technology changes quickly. With newer equipment (or even components) coming into plants almost daily, the skills of a maintenance workforce can be quickly dated. Some sources estimate that up to 80% of existing maintenance skills can be outdated within five years. The skills training program can utilize many resources, such as vocational schools, community colleges, or even vendor training. However, to be effective, the skills training program needs to focus on the needs of individual employees, and their needs should be tracked and validated.

12. Are the Maintenance Training Programs Effective?

This evaluation point focuses on the results of the skills training program. It deals with issues such as:
- Is there maintenance rework due to the technicians not having the skills necessary to perform the work correctly the first time?
- Is there ongoing evaluation of the employees skills versus the new technology or new equipment they are being asked to main tain or improve?
- Is there work being held back from certain employees because a manager or supervisor questions their ability to complete the work in a timely or quality manner?

If these questions uncover some weaknesses in the workforce, then it quickly shows that the maintenance skills training program is not effective. If this is the case, then a duty-task-needs analysis will highlight the content weaknesses in the current maintenance skills training program and provide areas for improvement to increase the versatility and utilization of the maintenance technicians.

13. Are Operators Involved in Maintenance Activities?

As the organization continues to make progress in the maintenance disciplines, it is time to investigate whether operator involvement is possible in some of the equipment management activities. There are many issues that need to be explored, from the types of equipment being operated, the operators-to-equipment ratios, and the skill levels of the operators, to contractual issues with the employees' union. In most cases, some level of activity is found in which the operators can be involved within their areas. If there are no obvious activities for operator involvement, then a re-evaluation of the activities will be necessary.

The activities the operators may be involved in may be basic or complex. It is partially determined by their current operational job requirements. Some of the more common tasks for operators to be involved in include, but are not necessarily limited to:

a. **Equipment Cleaning:** This may be simply wiping off their equipment when starting it up or shutting it down.

b. **Equipment Inspecting:** This may range from a visual inspection while wiping down their equipment to a maintenance inspections checklist utilized while making operational checks.

c. **Initiating Work Requests:** Operators may make out work requests for any problems (either current or developing) on their equipment. They would then pass these requests on to maintenance for entry into the work order system. Some operators will directly input work requests into a CMMS.

d. **Equipment Servicing:** This may range from simple running adjustments to lubrication of the equipment.

e. **Visual Systems:** Operators may use visual control techniques to inspect and to make it easier to determine the condition of their equipment.

Whatever the level of operator involvement, it should contribute to the improvement of the equipment effectiveness.

14. Are Operator-Performed Maintenance Tasks Effective?

Once the activities the operators are to be involved with has been determined, their skills to perform these activities need to be examined. The operators should be properly trained to perform any assigned tasks. The training should be developed in a written and visual format. Copies of the training materials should be used when the operators are trained and a copy of the materials given to the operators for their future reference. This will contribute to the commonality required for operators to be effective while performing these tasks. It should also be noted that certain regulatory organizations require documented and certified training for all employees (Lock Out Tag Out is an example).

Once the operators are trained and certified, they can begin performing their newly-assigned tasks. It is important for the operators to be coached for a short time to insure they have the full understanding of the hows and whys of the new tasks. Some companies have made this coaching effective by having the maintenance personnel assist with it. This allows for operators to receive background knowledge that they may not have gotten during the training.

15. Are Predictive Techniques Utilized?

Once the operators have begun performing some of their new tasks, some maintenance resources should be available for other activities. One area that should be explored is predictive maintenance. Some fundamental predictive maintenance techniques include:
- Vibration Analysis
- Oil Analysis
- Thermography
- Sonics

Plant equipment should be examined to see if any of these techniques will help reduce downtime and improve its service. Predictive technologies should not be utilized because they are technically advanced, but only when they contribute to improving the equipment effectiveness. The correct technology should be used to trend or solve the equipment problems encountered.

16. Are the PDM Tasks Effective?

If the proper PDM tools and techniques are used, there should be a decrease in the downtime of the equipment. Because the PDM program will find equipment wear before the manual PM techniques, the planning and scheduling of maintenance activities should also increase. In addition, some of the PM tasks that are currently being performed at the wrong interval should also be able to be adjusted. This will have a positive impact on the cost of the PM program. The increased efficiency of the maintenance workforce and the equipment should allow additional time to focus on advanced reliability techniques.

17. Are Reliability Techniques Being Utilized?

Reliability Engineering is a broad term that includes many engineering tools and techniques. Some common tools and techniques include:

a. Life Cycle Costing: - This technique allows companies to know the cost of their equipment, from when it was designed to the time of disposal.

b. R.C.M.: - Reliability Centered Maintenance is used to track the types of maintenance activities performed equipment to insure they are correct activities to be performed.

c. F.E.M.A.: - Failure and Effects Mode Analysis examines the way the equipment is operated and any failures incurred during the operation to find methods of eliminating or reducing the numbers of failures in the future.

d. Early Equipment Management and Design: This technique takes information on equipment and feeds it back into the design process, to ensure any new equipment is designed for maintainability and operability.

Using these and other reliability engineering techniques improve equipment performance and reliability to ensure competitiveness.

18. Are the Reliability Techniques Effective?

The proper utilization of reliability techniques will focus on eliminating repetitive failures on the equipment. While some reliability programs will also increase the efficiency of the equipment, this is usually the focus of TPM/OEE techniques. The elimination of the repetitive failures will increase the availability of the equipment. The effectiveness of the reliability techniques are measured by maximizing the uptime of the equipment.

19. Are TPM/ OEE Methodologies Being Utilized?

Are the TPM/OEE methodologies being utilized throughout the company? If they are not, then the TPM/OEE program needs to be examined for application in the company's overall strategy. If a TPM/OEE process exists, then it should be evaluated for gaps in performance or deficiencies in existing parts of the process. Once weaknesses are found, then steps should be taken to correct or improve these areas. Once the weaknesses are corrected and the goals are being achieved, then the utilization of the OEE for all equipment relate decisions is examined.

20. Is OEE Being Effectively Utilized?

The Overall Equipment Effectiveness provides a holistic look at how the equipment is utilized. If the OEE is too low, it indicates that the equipment is not performing properly and maximizing the return on investment in the equipment. Also, the upper limit for the OEE also needs to be understood. If a company were to focus on achieving the maximum OEE number, they may pay too much to ever recover the investment. If the OEE is not clearly understood, then additional training in this area must be provided. Once the OEE is clearly understood, then the focus can be switched to achieving the financial balance required to maximize a company's return on assets (ROA).

21. Does Total Cost Management Exist?

Once the equipment is correctly engineered, the next step is to understand how the equipment or process impacts the financial aspects of the company's business. Financial optimization considers all costs impacted when equipment decisions are made. For example, when calculating the timing to perform a preventive maintenance task, is the cost of lost production or downtime considered? Are wasted energy costs considered when cleaning heat exchangers or coolers? In this step, the equipment data collected by the company is examined in the context of the financial impact it has on the company's profitability. If the data exists and the information systems are in place to continue to collect the data, then financial optimization should be utilized. With this tool, equipment teams will be able to financially manage their equipment and processes.

22. Is Total Cost Management Utilized?

While financial optimization is not a new technique, most companies do not properly utilize it because they do not have the data necessary to make the technique effective. Some of the data required includes:
- MTBF (Mean Time Between Failure) for the equipment
- MTTR (Mean Time To Repair) for the equipment
- Downtime or lost production costs per hour
- A Pareto of the failure causes for the equipment
- Initial cost of the equipment
- Replacement costs for the equipment
- A complete and accurate work order history for the equipment

Without this data, financial optimization can not be properly conducted on equipment. Without the information systems in place to collect this data, a company will never have the accurate data necessary to perform financial optimization.

23. Are Continuous Improvement Techniques Utilized for Maintenance / Asset Management Decisions?

Once a certain level of proficiency is achieved in maintenance/ asset management, companies can begin to lose focus on their improvement efforts. They may even become complacent in their improvement efforts. However, there are excellent Continuous Improvement (CI) tools for examining even small problems. If new tools are constantly examined and applied to existing processes, all opportunities for improvement will be clearly identified and prioritized.

24. Are the CI Tools and Techniques Effective?

This question may appear to be subjective; however, improvements at this phase of maturity for a maintenance / reliability effort may be small and difficult to identify. However, the organizational culture of always looking for areas to improve is a true measure of the effectiveness of this step. As long as even small improvements in maintenance / reliability management are realized, this question should be answered "Yes."

25. Is Continuous Improvement Sought After in All Aspects of Maintenance / Asset Management?

When organizations reaches this stage, it will be clear that they are leaders in maintenance / reliability practices. Now, they will need continual focus on small areas of improvement. Continuous improvement means never getting complacent. It is the constant self-examination with the focus on how to become the best in the world at the company's business. Remember:

Yesterday's Excellence

is

Today's Standard

and

Tomorrow's Mediocrity

Maintenance Strategy Series Part 1

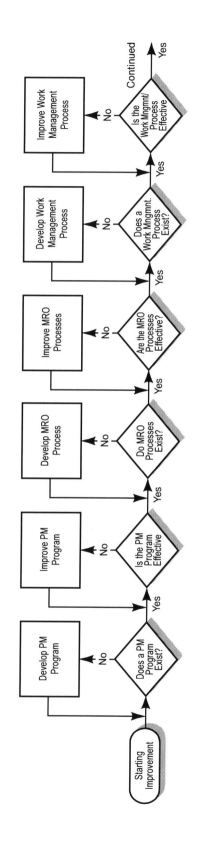

Maintenance Strategy Series Part 2

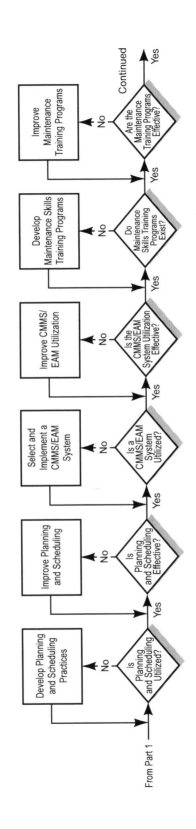

Maintenance Strategy Series Part 3

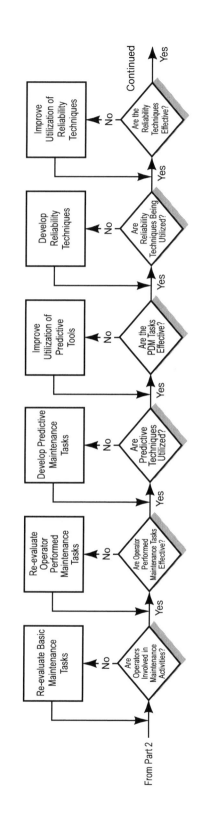

Maintenance Strategy Series Part 4

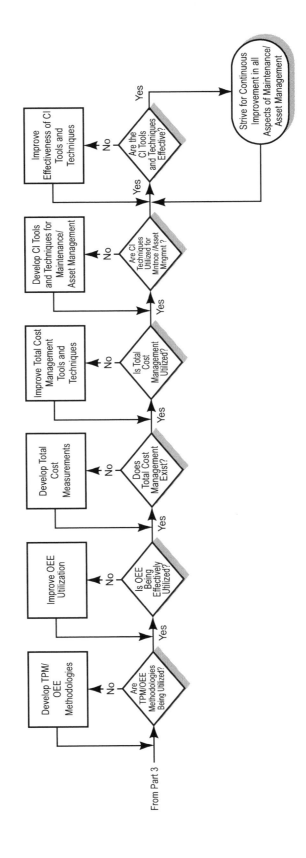

1

Introduction To CMMS/EAM

All industry segments today are in a fight to survive. Competition is found, not just on domestic levels, but also on international levels. In an effort to survive, all forms of competitive improvement programs are undergoing scrutiny by virtually every company. They are investigating any way to improve their key business processes.

One key business process on which many industries are now focusing their attention is the maintenance business function. Although this business function is often viewed as a necessary evil, with a continual focus on cost reduction; it is now being seen as an untapped opportunity for increased revenue generation.

Cost reduction in maintenance does not mean a reduction in the level of service or in the quality of service. It means a better control of the maintenance organization and the related areas. The concept of lean maintenance is to drive the waste out of the maintenance process. To properly control the maintenance of any facility, information is required about what is occurring. Manually gathering and analyzing this information requires a tremendous amount of effort and time.

In recognition of this, many of the progressive companies are developing and using computer programs geared toward control of the maintenance organization. These systems are referred to as computerized maintenance management systems (CMMS) or enterprise asset management systems (EAM). The CMMS / EAM system is designed to focus on gathering all maintenance-related data and filing it in the history of the proper asset, whether it is a piece of equipment, location, or a Building-Floor-Room locator (typically used in facilities). The flow diagram for a typical CMMS/EAM system is pictured in Figure 1-1.

Astute observers of the market for computerized maintenance management systems will have noticed that software vendors are beginning to call their products enterprise asset management (EAM) systems instead of CMMS.

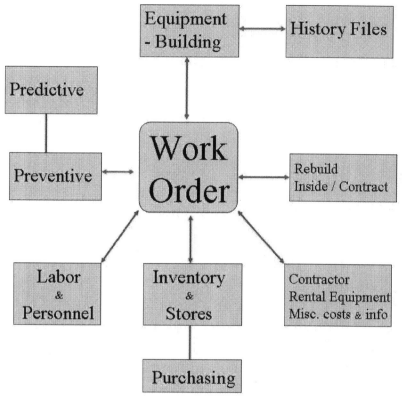

Figure 1-1 – A Typical CMMS Flow Diagram

To understand the reason for this change, one must be aware that many companies use enterprise resource planning (ERP) systems to manage all resources required to produce a product or provide a service. These systems are connected with businesses from order entry to order fulfillment. The majority of the ERP systems contain an EAM system as a module.

By contrast, a CMMS is used by the maintenance department to manage the maintenance function. Typically, a CMMS is independent of the main business system (usually an ERP system), and requires manual schedule integration to avoid conflicts.

When there are conflicts between ERP systems and a CMMS, it is often because of the failure to give sufficient emphasis to the maintenance function. In general, a company cannot successfully plan and schedule resources (assets) at an enterprise level without managing assets at that

EAM is more than CMMS

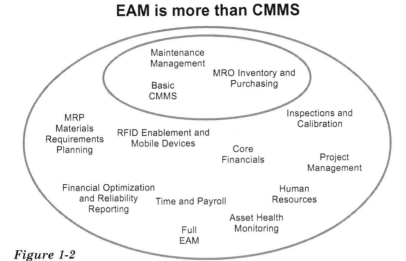

Figure 1-2

level. Most companies still manage assets at a department or, at best, a plant level.

Conflicts develop when, due to poor equipment availability, excess assets are purchased to ensure enough capacity to meet market demands. This strategy is uncontrolled, often resulting in excessive maintenance, repair, and operating costs as well as lower asset utilization. Excess (under-utilized) assets lower the return on assets (ROA), signaling to the investors that this company would be a poor investment.

The solution is to move beyond ERP and CMMS to an integrated EAM solution. EAM systems seek to manage a company's assets at an enterprise level to optimize their utilization, thereby maximizing the return on investment in the assets. EAM includes using real-time information from all parts of the company to balance the maintenance and operational needs in a financial equation that maximizes the shareholder's investment in the assets. In other words, EAM takes a process or asset-focused view of the entire business, as opposed to a product-focused view.

In summary, ERP systems entail planning based on capacity. EAM enables or delivers that capacity. Thus, EAM is more than maintenance management, and EAM software aims to be more than maintenance management software.

Another way to review the differences between any CMMS and an EAM system is to review the business functions they include. Whereas Figure 1-1 showed the basic outline for a CMMS, Figure 1-2 shows what a full EAM system includes. The basic CMMS focuses on managing maintenance, and on MRO inventory and purchasing. To have a full EAM system, areas such as company financials, human resources, time and payroll, and material requirements planning must be integrated. In addition, there are technical modules such as RFID and mobile devices, calibration devices, and real time asset health monitoring devices that must be integrated. When all of these are included, with a focus on properly managing the assets, then full EAM is achievable.

A third perspective on the value of the EAM is highlighted in Figure 1-3. This figure shows the CMMS module as the focal point for EAM. The other modules — such as financials, human resources, project-management, inventory and procurement, and manufacturing processes — all feed into the CMMS module. When performing maintenance on any of the equipment, the CMMS draws information from the inventory and purchasing data, which is typical in a corporate system. This step provides spare parts usage and cost information from the inventory and procurement module to the CMMS module.

Additional data, such as equipment run time or amount of product produced, are kept in the manufacturing system. Information such as certain run times or amounts of product produced sets a trigger in the CMMS to generate preventive maintenance activities.

The true EAM value potential can only be achieved by integrating all critical business processes

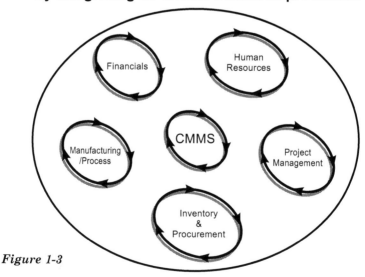

Figure 1-3

The integration with the financials module allows the CMMS to feed information to the financial system to be audited against budgets that have been established. The human resources module highlights personnel information such as skills and training information, so the right technician can be assigned the proper work. The project-management module helps track multiple work orders that are required to complete larger work projects, which are typically overhauls or construction type work.

Still another aspect of the EAM is how it manages the lifecycle phases of an asset. This impact is illustrated in Figure 1-4. At step 1, there is a decision to invest in a new asset. This may be as a replacement to an old asset, or it could be the investment in a new asset to begin a new product. In order to make the decision, there should be a financial study that highlights the investment required in the asset compared to the revenue that the new product launch will generate. If the equipment is being selected as a replacement, there still should be a financial study highlighting the benefits that will be achieved the purchase.

Once it has been determined that there will be an investment in a new asset, a performance specification for that asset will be generated (step 2). In addition to the performance of the asset, other elements must be specified including the asset's required life, maintenance requirements, and even construction material. After all this information is gathered, a

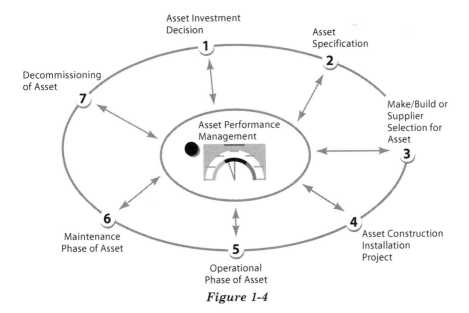

Figure 1-4

decision is made whether the equipment will be built internally or whether the specifications are sent to a supplier who will build the asset (step 3). If a decision is made for the supplier to build the equipment, then the specification information must become part of the contract.

Once the equipment is received, it will need to be installed (step 4). This step is typically part of a construction or installation project. During this step, the spare parts specifications are developed and the training of the operations and maintenance personnel take place.

Following this phase, which is typically called the commissioning phase, the equipment is ready to move into the operational phase (step 5). The operational phase of the equipment life cycle occurs when the equipment actually begins to produce product. Once the asset has actually begun to produce product, the maintenance phase also begins (step 6). It is during this phase that the majority of the costs of the equipment's life cycle are incurred. Studies have shown that up to 80% of the actual life cycle costs of an asset are incurred during the operational and maintenance phase of its life. However, this cost was actually specified during the asset specification and construction.

As the equipment continues to operate, it goes through various phases of its operational life, operating, and being maintained. Eventually, the equipment reaches the end of its useful life. It then moves into the decommissioning phase of the asset (step 7). At this time, it is useful to know the construction of the asset, and whether or not any hazardous materials will be involved in the decommissioning.

As can be seen, it is important to track all the information throughout the entire life cycle of the asset to optimize the investment in that asset. That is why it is necessary through all seven phases to track the performance of not just the asset, but of each department within the organization as it impacts the asset. Without this information, any decisions that are made will likely be inaccurate and create unnecessary costs.

Lifecycle costing is not a new concept. It has been practiced by companies since the late 1950s and early 1960s. However, in the 1970s, many organizations lost focus on lifecycle costing. As more and more organizations focused on quarter-to-quarter financials, they lost focus on the long-term value that operational strategies can bring to the bottom line. This led to production-only philosophies that measured throughput, but failed to measure the return on investment in the assets. With this focus, most organizations devolved to a reactive maintenance and asset management mentality.

Progression to EAM

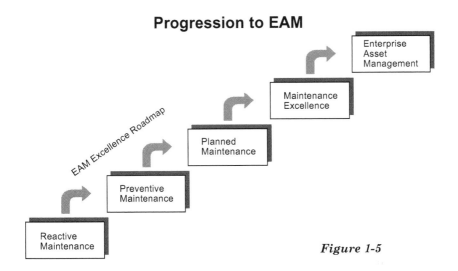

Figure 1-5

How can organizations reverse this by evolving from a reactive maintenance mentality to an enterprise asset management mentality? Figure 1-5 highlights this evolution.

If an organization is in a reactive maintenance mode, the first step for eliminating this mode is to install an effective preventive maintenance program in its place. With an effective preventive maintenance program, less than 20% of all maintenance resources should be deployed in a reactive mode. This stability allows for more effective utilization of maintenance resources by planning and scheduling.

The next step in the evolution moves from preventive maintenance in planned maintenance. In a planned maintenance mode, the labor productivity should increase to approximately 60%, which is typically double that which can be achieved in a reactive maintenance mode.

From a planned maintenance mode, the next step is to move into a maintenance excellence environment. An organization in the maintenance excellence mode optimizes all maintenance resources. Thus, it has very little waste of maintenance labor or maintenance materials. A maintenance excellence organization will utilize most of the tools that were highlighted in the "Maintenance Strategy Series" Preface at the front of this textbook. An organization achieving maintenance excellence may also be said to be a best practice organization.

This leaves the question, then, of how one moves from maintenance excellence to enterprise asset management? Maintenance excellence is practiced at a plant level; enterprise asset management is practiced at a corporate level. Therefore, all of the best practices of a maintenance excellence organization are disseminated from a corporate position until all maintenance organizations, in all plants, have achieved the maintenance excellence. With maintenance best practices focused on optimizing asset life cycles in each of their plants, a corporation can be said to have achieved enterprise asset management. Again, this progression is highlighted in Figure 1-5.

When considering EAM, one would have to ask who really does it. Most companies manage their assets at a plant or even a departmental level. For example, if maintenance and operations managers have agreed on a schedule for the next week, the schedule should be fixed. However, in many organizations, if shift managers for either maintenance or operations do not like what is scheduled for their shift, they change it. Could this be said to be enterprise asset management, or is it really departmental asset management? If an organization takes a product centric view, it can hardly be said that they are achieving enterprise asset management.

Consider for a moment corporate enterprise purchasing. When corporate purchasing contracts are negotiated, is it left up to the individual plants to choose which vendors they will utilize? Do they override the corporate or enterprise purchasing group in favor of a contract that they believe they can do better at negotiating? Of course not! When a company decides to utilize corporate or enterprise purchasing, the autonomy at the plant is removed. Should it be any different with enterprise asset management?

Consider, also, corporate or enterprise accounting. When corporate accounting practices are put into place, is it left up to each plant, or even each department, to decide for themselves which accounting practices and policies they will follow? Again, of course not. When a company decides to utilize corporate or enterprise accounting, the autonomy at the plant is removed. Should it be any different with enterprise asset management?

In each of these examples, there are substantial benefits to being standardized. In each of these examples, there is a return on investment for setting up corporate organizations to manage these business functions. Should it be any different for enterprise asset management? Why do most organizations fail to realize the benefits from standardizing asset management practices?

Previously, in Figure 1- 5, we considered the evolution from a reactive mode to maintenance excellence. If maintenance excellence was pictured as a maintenance maturity pyramid, it would appear as it does in Figure 1-6. A further description of this pyramid will appear in the next chapter. For the present, consider that each of these blocks represent a component of maintenance maturity. As an organization makes progress, it moves from the bottom of the pyramid to the top. However, this model is typically used at a plant level. If one were to evolve from a plant level towards achieving EAM, the figure would change as depicted in Fig. 1-7.

In this figure, the organization has a corporate maintenance excellence steering committee. (Note that the pyramids for each plant are identical to Figure 1-6.) This committee is typically made up of the maintenance managers from each of the plants. Each plant will be at different

Maintenance Maturity

Figures 1-6

Evolving to EAM - Part 1

Figures 1-7

stages on its journey to maintenance excellence. This means that each will have a different set of best practices in place.

It is up to the maintenance managers to meet periodically (perhaps once a month, but no less often than once a quarter) and discuss where they all are on their journey. It would be good for the location of the meeting to rotate from plant to plant. When specific managers host the meeting at their plant, they should be responsible for presenting the progress that they have made at their plant since the last visit. After the presentation, it would be good for the group to tour the plant, looking at the specific examples of the improvements that have been made. This allows each of the maintenance managers to see the benefits and the application of the maintenance improvement being presented. It is then easier for them to take these practices back to their plants and replicate them. Although this format allows the organization to share best practices, there is still more that is needed to achieve the EAM.

Figure 1-8 shows another addition to the diagram. At this point, a corporate maintenance director and an appropriate number of maintenance engineers have been added. This addition is important for continued progress because the maintenance managers at each plant already have a full-time job managing their maintenance departments. Although the monthly or quarterly meetings provide an excellent way to share best practices, there is no mechanism to institutionalize these practices. The corporate maintenance director would have the responsibility to collect all the best practices from each of the plants and to see that they are shared among the plants. With this focused effort, audited by the maintenance

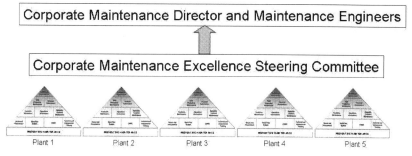

Evolving to EAM - Part 2

Corporate Maintenance Director and Maintenance Engineers

Corporate Maintenance Excellence Steering Committee

Plant 1   Plant 2   Plant 3   Plant 4   Plant 5

Figure 1-8

engineers, the best practices can be refined and quickly disseminated to the plant maintenance managers.

Adding the corporate maintenance director and the maintenance engineers does not replace the monthly or quarterly meeting. The corporate maintenance director must gather the information and see that it is communicated to all of the maintenance managers in a suitable format so that it can be applied in their plants. In addition, the corporate maintenance director must help the maintenance manager at each plant communicate the value of the improvement program to the plant manager and appropriate individuals on the management team. The corporate maintenance director, along with the maintenance engineers, should be adept at providing return on investment calculations for the maintenance improvement programs. This information will help the plant maintenance managers make progress on their journey to maintenance excellence.

Figure 1-9 shows a final addition to the diagram. In the previous diagram, the corporate maintenance director and the maintenance engineers were staff positions at the corporate level. In this position, they typically have no authority in the plants to enforce best practices. Figure 1-9 shows the corporate maintenance director and maintenance engineers reporting to an enterprise asset manager. Such individuals should have corporate authority. Organizationally, they may report to a chief operating officer or directly to a chief financial officer, or even to the chief execu-

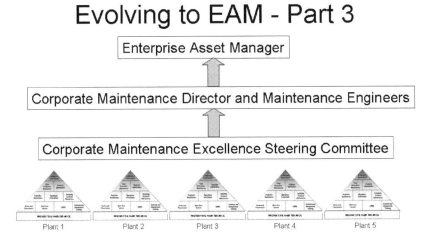

Figure 1-9

tive officer. Their primary responsibility is to oversee the utilization of all of the company's assets. This assignment goes beyond a typical plant manager to include areas such as overall equipment effectiveness, but focuses on the corporate-wide financial indicators. The primary performance indicator for the enterprise asset manager's job is generally return on assets (ROA), return on net assets (RONA), or return on fixed assets (ROFA).

When it comes to making decisions about plant assets, even the plant manager is subservient to this manager. This is similar to the plant manager complying with corporate accounting or corporate purchasing regulations. EAM managers are responsible for more than just maintenance and reliability (see Figure 1-10). They are empowered to control engineering as it relates to purchasing new equipment, retrofitting existing equipment, or decommissioning existing equipment. They control inventory and purchasing, when it comes to any practices or policies that impact the reliability and capacity of the corporate (plant) assets. They are also be responsible for interfacing with accounting, to ensure that no accounting practices such as depreciation, or tax rules such as expense versus capital, have any negative impact on the reliability and capacity of corporate assets.

It is only when a structure such as that pictured in Figure 1-9 is in place that true EAM is achieved.

EAM Manager

- Corporate authority
- Empowered to control usage of assets
- More than maintenance and reliability
    - Engineering
    - Inventory
    - Purchasing
    - Accounting
      As these relate to asset management

Figure 1-10

One may ask why have this discussion when the focus of the text-book is CMMS and EAM systems. A company's views of CMMS / EAM, and what they are trying to achieve long term, are critical to the selection and implementation of their system. If an organization is working with a small maintenance organization of ten or fewer maintenance employees and it is a stand alone department, then one of the smaller CMMS packages with good functionality will likely meet their needs.

However, if the organization is larger or is part of a multi-plant organization, then the choice of packages becomes more complex. The corporate direction may be to work all of the plants on a single system with integrated functionality. If this is the case, then the choice of the system may be made by a group consensus of all of the affected departments. The maintenance organization will want to make sure the functionality supports them if their direction is to evolve to EAM.

Only by understanding the 3-to-5 year strategic plan for the company can the correct system be selected, one that will enable all parts of the company to function efficiently.

2

MAINTENANCE STRATEGY ASSESSMENT

Understanding the Business Process

Note: The following material reviews the scope of the maintenance organization. (For a complete discussion of this topic, please see The Maintenance Strategy Series, Volume 3: Maintenance Work Management Processes.)

When computerizing any business process, it is important to understand the business process clearly. This is particularly true when the business process is maintenance. A complete maintenance strategy has many components. Understanding how an organization is going to develop its overall strategy is important in configuring and implementing a CMMS/EAM system. In addition, there are organizational considerations such as roles and responsibilities, and staffing levels. Finally, the organization's attitudes toward its assets and the maintenance function are critical to fully realizing any investment made in computerizing maintenance management. This chapter will be divided into the following three sections:
- Maintenance strategy components
- Organizational issues
- Organizational attitudes

Maintenance Management Strategy Components

What components comprise a comprehensive maintenance (asset) management strategy? The list includes (but is not be limited to) the following:

1. Preventive Maintenance
2. Inventory and Procurement

15

3. Work Flow and Controls
4. CMMS Usage
5. Technical and Interpersonal Training
6. Operational Involvement
7. Predictive Maintenance
8. Reliability Centered Maintenance
9. Total Productive Maintenance
10. Financial Optimization
11. Continuous Improvement

There is a structure to the maintenance (asset) management function. It is best compared to a pyramid, as shown in Figure 2-1. In this figure, it is apparent that a foundation must be in place to build a successful maintenance management process. That foundation is preventive maintenance. Once it is in place, stores, work flow, CMMS, and training form the next level. The operations involvement, predictive maintenance, and RCM techniques build on this level. With sufficient data, the organization can focus on its asset strategy in TPM and optimize its financials. Once that level is achieved, all that is left is the continuous improvement loop of self-evaluation and benchmarking.

Maintenance Maturity

Figure 2-1

All of these initiatives are building blocks for the maintenance (asset) management process. A brief examination of each will show its importance to the maintenance (asset) management process.

1.   Preventive Maintenance

The preventive maintenance program is the key to any successful asset management program. It reduces the amount of reactive maintenance to a level that the other initiatives in the asset management process can be effective. However, most companies in the United States have problems keeping their PM programs focused. In fact, surveys have shown that only 20% of U.S. companies believe their PM programs are effective.

This finding indicates that most companies need to focus on the basics of maintenance if they are to achieve any type of asset management process. Effective preventive maintenance activities would enable a company to achieve a ratio of 80 proactive maintenance to 20% (or less) reactive maintenance. Once the ratios are at least at this level, the other initiatives in the asset management process become more effective. From the financial perspective, reactive maintenance typically costs 2–4 times what proactive maintenance costs, due to the inherent inefficiencies. Because the asset management process is focused on ROI, it is critical for all companies to have a successful PM program as a foundation.

2.   Inventory and Procurement

The inventory and procurement programs must focus on providing the right parts at the right time for the asset repairs and maintenance. The goal is to have enough spare parts, without having too many spare parts. The interdependency between the asset management initiatives becomes apparent: No inventory and procurement process can cost-effectively service a reactive maintenance process. But, if the majority of maintenance work can be planned several weeks in advance, the practices within the inventory and procurement process can be optimized.

What level of performance is typical in companies today? Many companies see service levels below 90%, which means stockouts run greater than 10% of requests made. This level of service leaves customers (maintenance) fending for themselves, stockpiling personal stores, and circumventing the standard procurement channels to obtain their materials. This is not done for personal reasons, but rather because they want to provide service to their customer (operations or facilities). It is really a self-defense mechanism.

In order to prevent this situation, it is necessary to institute the type of stores controls that will allow the service levels to reach 95–97%, with complete accuracy of the data. When this level of stores and procurement performance is achieved, the next step in asset management is ready to be taken.

3. *Work Flows and Controls*

This initiative in asset management involves documenting and tracking the maintenance work that is performed. It involves the use of a work order system to initiate, track, and record all maintenance and engineering activities. The work may start as a request that needs approval. Once approved, the work is planned, then scheduled, performed, and finally recorded. Unless the discipline is in place and enforced to follow this process, data is lost and true analysis can never be performed.

Unfortunately, many organizations record only a small part of their maintenance and engineering actions; therefore, much data is lost. When it comes time to perform an analysis of the data, the analysis is incomplete and inaccurate. Management doesn't support the decisions made, based on the data, and further degradation of their confidence in the maintenance department occurs.

The solution requires complete use of the work order system to record all maintenance and engineering activities. Unless the data is tracked from work request through completion, the data is fragmented and useless. If 100% of all maintenance and engineering activities are tracked through the work order system, then planning and scheduling can be effective.

Planning and scheduling requires someone to perform the following activities:

- Review the work submitted
- Approve the work
- Plan the work activities
- Schedule the work activities
- Record the completed work activities

Unless a disciplined process is followed for these steps, the increases in productivity and reduced equipment downtime never occur. These results leave the perception that maintenance planning is a clerical function. This perception makes the planning function vulnerable to the first cuts when any types of reduction in overhead costs are examined. At least

80% of all maintenance work should be planned on a weekly basis. In addition, the schedule compliance should be at least 90% on a weekly basis.

4. *CMMS Usage*

In most companies, sufficient data is accumulated by the maintenance and engineering functions to require the computerization of the data flow. This facilitates the collection, processing, and analysis of the data. The usage of the Computerized Maintenance Management System (CMMS) has become popular in most countries around the world. This software manages the functions discussed previously, and provides support for Asset Management.

CMMSs have been utilized for almost a decade in some countries with very mixed results. A recent U.S. survey showed the majority of companies utilizing less than 30% of their CMMS/EAM system functionality. What does this mean for these companies? It means that the data they collect is highly suspect and probably highly inaccurate. Unless this problem is corrected, these companies will never be able to achieve true asset management, because there will be no method of tracking asset costs and calculating ROI.

5. *Technical and Interpersonal Training*

This function of maintenance insures that the technicians working on the equipment have the technical skills that are required to understand and maintain the equipment. Additionally, those involved in the maintenance functions must have the interpersonal skills to be able to communicate with other departments in the company. They must also be able to work in a team or natural work group environment. Without these skills, there is little possibility of maintaining the current status of the equipment. Furthermore, the probability of ever making any improvement in the equipment is inconceivable.

Although there are exceptions, the majority of companies today lack the technical skills within their organizations to maintain their equipment. In fact, studies have shown that almost 1/3 of the adult population in the United States is functionally illiterate or just marginally better. When these figures are coupled with the lack of apprenticeship programs available to technicians, the specter of a workforce where the technology of the equipment has exceeded the skills of the technicians that operate or maintain it has become a reality.

6. *Operational Involvement*

Operational involvement requires the operations, production, or facilities departments to take ownership of their equipment to the extent that they are willing to support the maintenance and engineering departments' efforts. The aspects of involvement vary from company to company. The involvement activities may include some of the following:

- Inspecting equipment prior to start up
- Making out work requests for maintenance
    (This includes building occupants requesting work)
- Recording breakdown or malfunction data for equipment
- Performing some basic equipment service (e.g., lubrication)
- Performing routine adjustments on equipment
- Performing maintenance activities (supported by central maintenance)

The extent to which operations, production, and facilities are involved in maintenance activities may depend on the complexity of the equipment, the skills of the individuals, or even union agreements. The goal should always be to free up some of the maintenance and engineering resources so that they can concentrate on more advanced asset management techniques.

7. *Predictive Maintenance*

Once the maintenance and engineering resources have been freed up by the operational involvement, they should be refocused on the predictive technologies that apply to the assets. For example, rotating equipment is a natural fit for vibration analysis, electrical equipment for thermography, and so on. In some cases, the devices monitoring the asset may be connected to a building automation system, a distributed control system, or a PLC system, and all parameters are monitored in a real time environment.

The focus is not to purchase all the technology available, but to investigate and purchase technology that solves or mitigates chronic equipment problems that exist. The predictive inspections should be planned and scheduled utilizing the same techniques that are used to schedule the preventive tasks. All data should be recorded in or interfaced to the CMMS.

8. *Reliability Centered Maintenance*

If the data is recorded, Reliability Centered Maintenance (RCM) techniques are now applied to the preventive and predictive efforts to optimize the programs. If a particular asset is environmentally sensitive, safety related, or extremely critical to the operation, then the appropriate PM/PDM techniques are decided upon and utilized.

If an asset is going to restrict or impact the production or operational capacity of the company, then another level of PM/PDM activities is applied with a cost ceiling in mind. If the asset was allowed to fail and the cost would be the expense to replace or rebuild the asset, then another level of PM/PDM activities would be specified. There is always the possibility that it is more economical to allow some assets run to failure, and this option is considered in RCM.

The RCM tools require data to be effective and it is for this reason that the RCM process is utilized after the organization has reached a level of maturity that insures accurate and complete asset data.

9. *Total Productive Maintenance*

Total Productive Maintenance (TPM) is an operational philosophy, where everyone in the company understands that in some way their job performance impacts the performance of the asset. For example, operations understands the true capacity of the equipment and does not run it beyond design specifications, creating unnecessary breakdowns. The purchasing department always buys spare parts to the correct specifications, not trying to save a small amount while creating breakdowns because the parts didn't last as long as they should.

TPM is like Total Quality Management. The only change is that instead of companies focusing on their product, the focus shifts to their assets. All of the tools and techniques used to implement, sustain, and improve the total quality effort can be utilized in TPM.

10. *Financial Optimization*

Financial optimization is a statistical technique that combines all of the relevant data about an asset, such as:

- Downtime cost
- Maintenance cost
- Lost efficiency cost
- Quality cost

and balances out financially optimized decisions, such as:

- When do you take the asset off line for maintenance?
- Do you repair or replace an asset?
- How many critical spare parts should you carry?
- What should be the max-min levels on routine spare parts?

Financial optimization requires accurate data because making these types of decisions incorrectly could have a devastating effect on a company's competitive position. By the time a company reaches a level of sophistication where this technique can be utilized, it is approaching the pinnacle of the asset management pyramid.

11. Continuous Improvement

Continuous Improvement is best epitomized by the expression, "Best is the Enemy of Better." Continuous Improvement in asset care is an ongoing program of evaluation, constantly looking for the little things that can make a company more competitive. One of the key tools for continuous improvement is benchmarking. There are several types of benchmarking, but process benchmarking is one of the most successful. Process benchmarking examines specific processes in maintenance, compares the processes to companies that have mastered those processes, and maps changes to improve the specific process.

The key to benchmarking is the self-evaluation. A company must know its current status before it tries to benchmark with other companies. Without this knowledge, it is impossible to get an accurate comparison of the benchmarked process.

Assessing Maintenance Organizational Issues

The following evaluation may be used in assessing the "As-Is – To-Be" condition of a maintenance organization. It is designed not only to assess the current status, but also to help the organization understand some of the developmental options that they may wish to develop in the future. The questions are designed to focus attention on areas that are sometimes overlooked in the implementation of a CMMS / EAM system.

Section 1: Maintenance Organizations

1. Is the maintenance organizational chart current?

2. Are job descriptions available for all positions?

3. What is the maintenance supervisor to hourly maintenance employee ratio?

4. What is the maintenance planner to hourly maintenance employee ratio?

5. Are maintenance organizational assignments fully documented?

6. Are the maintenance organization's effort and attitude acceptable?

7. Are maintenance shop/work area locations acceptable?

8. Are maintenance shop/work area layouts acceptable?

9. Are maintenance tools/equipment quality and quantity acceptable?

10. What percent of maintenance personnel are tied to a pay incentive plan based on output?

Section 2: Training Programs for Maintenance

1. Is supervisory training current and acceptable?

2. Is planner training current and acceptable?

3. What are the details of planner training?

4. Are the general quality and productivity training acceptable?

5. Is maintenance craft training acceptable?

6. What are the maintenance training intervals?

7. Is the format of maintenance training acceptable?

8. What are the training program instructors' skills?

9. Are the quality and skill level of the maintenance work force acceptable?

10. Are the quality and skill level of the supervisory group acceptable?

Section 3: Maintenance Work Orders

1. What percent of maintenance man-hours are reported to a work order?

2. What percent of maintenance materials are charged against a work order number when issued?

3. What percent of total jobs performed by maintenance are covered by work orders?

4. What percent of the work orders processed in the system are tied to an equipment/asset number?

5. What percent of the work orders are opened under a priority that would be identified as emergency or urgent?

6. What percent of the work orders are available for historical data analysis?

7. What percent of the work orders are checked by a qualified individual for work quality and completeness?

8. What percent of the work orders are closed within eight weeks from the date requested?

9. What percent of the work orders are generated from the preventive maintenance inspections?

10. What are the categories available for tracking for work orders?

Section 4: Maintenance Planning and Scheduling

1. What percent of non-emergency work orders are completed within four weeks of the initial request?

2. Work order planning is performed for what percent of the work?

3. What percent of planned work orders are experiencing delays due to poor or incomplete plans?

4. Who is responsible for planning the work orders?

5. Are maintenance job schedules issued?

6. Are maintenance and production/facilities scheduling meetings held?

7. By what categories is the backlog of maintenance work available?

8. When the job is completed, who reports the actual time, material, downtime, and other information?

9. What percent of the time are actual measures compared to the estimates for monitoring planning effectiveness?

10. What is the reporting relationship between planners and supervisors?

Section 5: Preventive Maintenance

1. What activities does the preventive maintenance program include?

2. What percent of the PM inspection/task checklists are checked to insure completeness?

3. What percent of the plant's critical equipment is covered by a preventive maintenance program?

4. What percent of the PM program is checked against an equipment item's history annually to insure good coverage?

5. What percent of the PMs are completed within one week of the due date?

6. What determines the frequency of a PM inspection or task/service interval?

7. What percent of the inspections/tasks include safety information, detailed inspection instructions, material requirements, and labor estimates?

8. What percent of the corrective action work orders are generated from the PM inspection program?

9. On what percent of the program are PM actuals and results checked annually for time and material estimate accuracy?

10. Who is responsible for performing preventive maintenance tasks?

Section 6: Maintenance Inventory and Purchasing

1. What percent of the time are materials in stores when required by the maintenance organization?

2. What percent of the items in inventory appear in the maintenance stores catalog?

3. Who controls what are stocked as maintenance inventory items?

4. Who produced the maintenance stores catalog?

5. For what percent of the stores items is the aisle/bin location specified?

6. What percent of the maintenance stores items are issued to a work order or account number upon leaving the store?

7. For what percent of the inventory are maximum and minimum levels for the maintenance stores items specified?

8. What percent of the critical maintenance material is stocked in the warehouse or in a location readily accessible when the material is required?

9. What percent of the time are maintenance stores inventory levels updated daily upon receipt of materials?

10. What percent of the items are checked for at least one issue every six months?

Section 7: Maintenance Automation

1. What percentage of all maintenance operations utilize a CMMS?

2. What percentage of maintenance activities are planned and scheduled through a CMMS?

3. What percentage of the maintenance inventory and purchasing functions are performed in the system?

4. Are the CMMS and the production scheduling system integrated?

5. Are the CMMS and the payroll/ timekeeping system integrated?

6. Are the CMMS and the financial/accounting system integrated?

7. What percent of the maintenance personnel are using the system for their job functions with a high level of proficiency?

8. Are CMMS data structured and maintained to facilitate reporting?

9. Are CMMS data utilized, on a regular basis, to make cost effective management decisions?

10. Are CMMS data used to verify progressive ROI?

Section 8: Operations/Facilities Involvement

1. What percent of operations personnel generate work order requests?

2. What percent of facilities personnel generate work order requests?

3. How is the operations work order priority set for maintenance?

4. How is the facility work order priority set for maintenance?

5. Are operations/operators responsible and involved in the upkeep and performance of assets?

6. What activities are operators trained and certified to perform?

7. What percent of the time do operators follow-up and sign-off on completed work orders?

8. What percent of the time do facilities personnel follow-up and sign-off on completed work orders?

9. Is maintenance included in production/process scheduling meetings?

10. Does asset-focused communication exist among maintenance, operations, engineering, and facilities personnel?

Section 9: Maintenance Reporting

1. What percent of the time are the maintenance reports distributed on a timely basis to the appropriate personnel?

2. What percent of the time are the reports distributed within one

day of the end of the time period specified in the report?

3. Which of the following equipment reports do you produce?

   A. Equipment downtime in order from highest to lowest total hours (weekly or monthly)

   B. Equipment downtime in order from highest to lowest in total lost production dollars (weekly or monthly)

   C. Maintenance cost for equipment in order from highest to lowest (weekly or monthly)

   D. MTTR and MTBF for equipment

4. Which of the following preventive maintenance reports do you produce?

   A. PM overdue report in order from oldest to most recent

   B. PM cost per equipment item in descending order

   C. PM hours verses total maintenance hours per item expressed as a percentage

   D. PM costs verses total maintenance costs per equipment item expressed as a percentage

5. Which of the following personnel reports do you produce?

   A. Time report showing hours worked by employee divided by work order

   B. Time report showing hours worked by craft in each department/area

   C. Time report showing total hours spent by craft on emergency /preventive/normal work

   D. Time report showing total overtime hours compared to regular hours

6. Which of the following planning reports do you produce?

    A. Total work order costs estimated versus total work order actual costs by individual work order, by supervisor, or by craft

    B. A backlog report showing the total hours ready to schedule versus the craft capacity per week

    C. A planning efficiency report showing the hours and materials planned versus the actual hours and materials used per work order

    D. A planning effectiveness report showing the number of jobs closed out that were 20% over or under the labor or material estimates by planner and supervisor

7. Which of the following scheduling reports do you produce?

    A. Hours worked as scheduled compared to actual hours worked

    B. Weekly crew or craft capacity averaged for the last 20 weeks

    C. Total number of maintenance work orders scheduled compared to the actual number of work orders completed

    D. Number of work orders spent on preventive maintenance compared to emergency maintenance and normal maintenance

8. Which of the following inventory reports do you produce?

    A. Stock catalog by alphabetical and numerical listing

    B. Inventory valuation report

    C. Inventory performance report showing stockouts and level of service, turnover rate, etc.

    D. Inventory where used report

9. Which of the following purchasing reports do you produce?

   A. Vendor performance showing promised and actual delivery dates

   B. Price performance, showing the quoted and actual prices

   C. Buyer or purchasing agent performance report

   D. Non-stock report showing all direct buys for items not carried in stock for a specified period

10. Which of the following administrative reports do you produce?

   A. Monthly maintenance costs versus monthly maintenance budget with a year-to-date total

   B. Comparison of labor and material costs as a percentage of total maintenance costs

   C. Total costs of outside contractor usage broken down by contractor/project

   D. Maintenance cost per unit of production (or by square foot for facilities)

Section 10 Predictive Maintenance

1. Does the predictive maintenance program include vibration analysis?

2. Does the predictive maintenance program include thermography?

3. Does the predictive maintenance program include oil analysis?

4. Does the predictive maintenance program utilize sonic techniques?

5. Is condition-based monitoring included in the predictive maintenance program?

6. Is the predictive maintenance system tied into the CMMS?

7. Is the predictive maintenance data used to generate preventive/ corrective maintenance work orders?

8. Are personnel exclusively assigned to the predictive maintenance program?

9. Is predictive work included as part of the weekly work schedule?

10. Is predictive maintenance data used to improve asset performance and life expectancy?

Section 11: Reliability Engineering

1. Does the organization have a reliability engineering attitude/ mentality?

2. Is complete and accurate asset data available for Reliability Centered Maintenance analysis?

3. Is the RCM methodology used to adjust/refine the PM/PDM program?

4. How often is an RCM analysis conducted on all assets?

5. Is the work order history accurate in tracking the causes of failures?

6. Are failures clearly identified?

7. Is failure analysis conducted using analysis tool such as why tree, fishbone, and Pareto, to assure accuracy and consistency of the effort?

8. Are dedicated personnel permanently assigned to maintain the RCM program?

9. Does management view RCM as a value-added activity?

10. Are methods in place for measuring the effectiveness of the reliability engineering effort?

Section 12: Maintenance – General Practices

1. Is the total organization focused on asset utilization/optimization?
2. Is the maintaining function perceived as value added by the organization?
3. Is the maintenance data collection system utilized by the whole organization?
4. Are the operators used for first-line maintenance functions?
5. Is overall equipment effectiveness calculated on key assets, processes, and facilities?
6. Are operational decisions made by taking into account equipment reliability/availability?
7. Have the right soft skills training classes (e.g., communications, leadership) been conducted for appropriate personnel?
8. Have the right technical training classes been conducted for appropriate personnel?
9. Does the maintenance program comply with regulator requirements and programs?
10. Are the financial effects of equipment availability/reliability understood and communicated to everyone?

Section 13: Financial Optimization

1. Is downtime duration consistently tracked?
2. Is the downtime cost clearly identified for key assets, processes, and facilities?
3. Are downtime causes accurately and consistently tracked?
4. Are maintenance costs clearly and accurately tracked?
5. Are other contributing costs (e.g., energy, quality, contractors) available for analysis?
6. Are total operational costs compared when making decisions?

7. Are efficiency loss costs available and accurate?

8. Is there a dedicated individual or team assigned to analyze financial costs?

9. Are stores and purchasing costs accurately tracked?

10. Is the financial information readily available?

Section 14: Asset Care Continuous Improvement

1. Is there visible management support for continuous improvement efforts?

2. Does the organization support continuous improvement efforts?

3. If the company has recently downsized, how has downsizing affected the organization?

4. Has there been good support of past improvement efforts?

5. What is the spirit of cooperation between plant management and labor?

6. What groups in the organization are focused on continuous improvement?

7. Does management support ongoing training designed to enhance employee skills?

8. Do continuous improvement efforts focus on ROI?

9. Are continuous improvement efforts tied to reliability engineering?

10. Do competitive forces influence continuous improvement efforts?

Section 15: Maintenance Contracting

1. What processes compose the contract request process?

2. Who is responsible for the contracting of work?

3. Who does the approved list of contractors include?

4. Who does the owner provide for the supervision for contracted field execution?

5. Who is responsible for contractor safety?

6. What is the computerized contracting functionality on the front end of the process?

7. What is the computerized contracting functionality on the back end of the process?

8. How is the contracting system connected to the CMMS / EAM system?

9. What is the relationship between the site personnel and the contractor personnel?

10. How effective is the invoicing/cost tracking process?

Section 16: Document Management

1. What is the level of computerization of the site's document management system?

2. What is the percentage of drawings included in the system?

3. When does the site plan to migrate to a fully functional and utilized document management system?

4. Do document control procedures and associated work process exist?

5. What is the level of usage of the system by the personnel at the site?

6. Does the current system have detailed indexing and search capabilities?

7. How accessible is the system for the users?

8. What is the quality and level of document version control?

9. What is the percentage of drawings that have been updated in the last year?

Maintenance Organizational Attitudes

This section examines the organization's overall attitude and understanding of the maintenance business function. A fully functional maintenance management organization requires an understanding of other management groups within the organization. Some of the issues are common management functions related to developing a business. For example, four general responsibilities of business development are:

1. Establish the purpose of the organization.
2. Determine measurable objectives to support the purpose.
3. Set permissible variance for the objectives.
4. Determine the actions necessary to maintain the organization within the variance.

Although these statements are generic, the application needs to be made to the maintenance business. The reason is that maintenance is the last opportunity some organizations will have to achieve their "World Class" programs. For example, how can Just-In-Time, Total Quality Control, or Total Employee Involvement programs work with unreliable or poorly-maintained equipment? Consider the following examples.

How can Just-In-Time programs work with equipment availability of 60%?

Current management philosophy is to invest in excess equipment or redundant assets to assure sufficient capacity to support the Just-In-Time program. However, what would happen if we maintained the equipment to assure 100% availability? What would the savings be in capital investment? It would be greater than the maintenance cost that would be required to assure 100% availability! But which course do organizations with immature attitudes toward maintenance management choose? Examine a good cross-section of organizations in this country and you will see an excess of redundant equipment, which are unnecessary capital expenditures.

What About Total Quality Control Programs?

How many of the quality circles contain skilled members of the maintenance staff? In cases where companies do include maintenance as part of the team, they often fail to use maintenance to provide them with

Maintenance Management Maturity Grid

Measurement Category	Stage 1 Uncertain	Stage 2 Developing	Stage 3 Transitional	Stage 4 Maturing	Stage 5 Best Practice
Corporate/Plant Management Attitude	No comprehension of maintenance prevention; fix it when it breaks or "If it isn't broken don't fix it," philosophies prevail	Recognizes that maintenance policies and practices could be improved, but is unwilling to fund improvements	Learns more about ROI, becomes more interested and supportive in asset/maintenance improvements	Participative attitude; recognizes management support is mandatory for effective asset/maintenance management policies	Includes asset/maintenance management as a key component of their company's overall enterprise strategy
Maintenance Organizational Status	REACTIVE Works on equipment when it fails, otherwise very little maintenance productivity; when not firefighting, technicians are kept busy with low priority "fill-in" work	AWAKENING: Still reactive but rebuilds major components and has spares available when failures occur to make replacements faster; preventive maintenance efforts fragmented	PREVENTIVE: Uses routine inspections, lubrication, adjustments, and minor service to improve MTBF and reduce equipment failures	PREDICTIVE: Utilizes Techniques such as vibration analysis, thermography, spectrography, NDT, sonics, etc., to monitor condition, allowing for proactive replacement and problem solving instead of allowing failures to occur	PRODUCTIVE: Combine prior techniques with operator involvement to free up maintenance technicians to conduct RCA and RCM analysis and other asset/maintenance improvement activities
Percentage (%) of Maintenance Resources Wasted	30+%	20-30%	10-20%	5-10%	Less than 5%
Maintenance problem solving	Asset/Equipment problems fought as they occur; no proactive equipment problem analysis conducted - no failure analysis utilized	Short-range fixes for asset/equipment problems are utilized, elementary failure analysis is used occassionally, but no discipline to the effort	Asset/equipment problems solved by input from maintenance, operations, and engineering teams; structured procedures employed	Asset/Equipment problems are anticipated utilizing RCM techniques; strong team problem-solving disciplines are utilized	Proactive asset/equipment strategies are standardized; if problems occur, they are solved and processes and procedures are adjusted to eliminate future occurances

Maintenance Technician Qualification and Training	Poor quality workmanship accepted; rigid craft lines; craft skills outdated, maintenance skills training viewed as unnecessary expense, time in grade determines pay, low worker turnover/ apathy	Worker's lack of skills linked to breakdowns; trade/ craft lines questioned, skills obsolescence Identified; training needs recognized, traditional pay questioned	D.I.R.T.F. Philosophy developed; expanded/ shared job roles, a few "critical skills" developed, training expenses reimbursed, new pay level for targeted skills, increased turnover/ fear of change	Quality work expected; Zero Maintenance rework is a goal; "multiskill" job roles; skills up to date and tracked; training required and provided; pay for competency progression	Pride and profession-alism permeates work force; technicians skilled for future needs: Operators trained by maintenance, ongoing training; percent of pay based on plant productivity; low employee turnover/ high enthusiasm
Maintenance Information and Improvement Actions	Maintenance tries to keep records, disciplines are not enforced, incomplete and poor quality data available	A manual or computerized work order system is used by maintenance, little or no planning and scheduling - data still inaccurate	A manual or computerized work order system is used by maintenance, operations, engineering, planners used, scheduling enforced	A computerized asset / maintenance management system is used by all parts of the company, information is reliable and accurate	An Enterprise Asset Management system is integrated into the corporate operation
Summation of Company Maintenance Management Position	"We don't know why the equipment breaks down, that is what we pay maintenance for. Sure, our downtime is high, but that is a maintenance problem."	"Do our competitors have these kind of problems with their equipment? Asset/ Equipment Downtime is making us uncompetitive!"	"With the financial impact of maintenance understood by management, we can begin to obtain resources to identify and solve asset/ equipment related problems."	"Everyone is committed to asset/ maintenance management as a routine part of our corporate strategy. We can't compete in our marketplace with poorly designed, operated, or maintained equipment."	"We don't expect asset or equipment problems and are surprised when they occur; Asset/ maintenance management contributes to our RONA and adds value to the shareholders!"

Figure 2-2

any competitive advantage. Consider this question: What percentage of all your organization's quality problems are related to maintenance? 20–50%? Even more? How can U.S. companies expect to compete in a world market that already recognizes the valuable contribution maintenance can make to their competitive efforts? If organizations don't use this tool in their efforts to improve quality, they will be at a major disadvantage.

How About the Maintenance Effect on Total Employee Involvement?

What are employees' attitudes when they recognize a problem that management refuses to acknowledge, much less act on? As taught by any TEI expert or consultant, management's refusal to recognize or correct a problem leads to ineffectiveness of the program. Many problems that TEI teams can identify are related to the lack of good maintenance fundamentals. How will these programs eventually end if management refuses to recognize and act on good maintenance fundamentals? The results could be disastrous. Without skilled maintenance technicians to provide answers to equipment related problems, organizations will lose their competitive edge.

The method to raise management's awareness of the value of maintenance to the organization is to show the value of maintenance in a bottom-line oriented manner. Using financial information to assist in making maintenance-related decisions is one of the most effective ways to raise organizational awareness. The key to this is to view maintenance expenditures in the view of Total Cost.

When examining the cost of a maintenance action, plot it against the cost of non-maintenance, such as:

- Lost production cost
- Costs required to make up lost production
- Quality costs, particularly rework and scrap energy costs
- Customer satisfaction costs
- Delayed delivery penalties
- Lost customer costs
- Environmental penalty costs
- Safety penalty costs
- Devaluation of capital assets

It is only when organizations understand the impact of maintenance or the lack of maintenance (the Total Cost Concept) that the desire to be competitive will be achieved.

Maintenance Management Maturity Grid

Maintenance improvement requires a long-term commitment. The Japanese realize and openly explain that a TPM program takes three-to-five years of implementation. Organizations in the United States will have to be willing to put the same kind of effort into implementation of maintenance improvement programs. Organizational management must realize that PM, PDM, TPM, and CMMS are not part of the program-of-the-month club offerings. Maintenance improvement requires commitment and time to achieve results.

What is required is a pathway, one that can develop maintenance improvement programs by raising organizational understanding. A tool developed to help facilitate the communications necessary to achieve this understanding is the Maintenance Management Maturity Grid shown in Figure 2-2. This grid was developed from concepts used in The Quality Management Maturity Grid published by Phillip Crosby (Quality Is Free, McGraw-Hill Book Company, 1979).

The grid is divided into stages and categories. The stages are the steps organizational management progresses through on the path to maturity. When using the grid to evaluate the organization, managers will not miss which stage they are in by more than 1 unless they are using the "Ostrich" method of managing. Organizations that have used this grid to evaluate themselves have mailed out copies to various departments. Each department then circled the stage where they believed the organization was in each category. They then compiled the results and averaged the scores for the organization. They used the total results to build a maintenance improvement program for the organization.

The resulting program is more readily accepted by the organization because all departments are included and understand the goals. The Maintenance Management Maturity Grid not only helps organizations evaluate their present status, but also understand the steps required to reach the next stage and also the derived benefits of improvement.

Categories

The measurement categories are divided into seven sections. Each section addresses a key part of an organization's maintenance program. The responses under each category are typical of the maturity of the organization.

1. Corporate/Plant Management Attitude

This category reflects how upper management views the maintenance organization. This category is important because no maintenance improvement program ever will succeed without strong management support. Achieving this support will require education. This education will focus on the financial impact maintenance has on the organization. Because upper management understands the factors affecting the bottom line, all communication should be translated into this language.

2. Maintenance Organization Status

This category examines the type of attitude that maintenance uses to approach its work. Many organizations use the "fire-fighting" approach to maintenance. The number of organizations diminishes as your move across the grid into the successive stages. This is evident because there are very few organizations practicing productive maintenance in North America.

3. Percentage of Maintenance Resources Wasted

This category relates to the previous one, because the more reactive an organization is, the more resources it wastes. Studies show that reactive organizations waste 30% or more of the controllable maintenance resources. As maintenance disciplines become effective, the wastes are reduced. Good planning and scheduling practices coupled with effective work order systems help to eliminate wastes.

4. Maintenance Problem Solving

This area is the trouble shooting part of the maintenance organization. Reactive organizations do not use effective problem-solving techniques because they do not have time. As maintenance becomes more controlled, more time is allocated to cause and effect analysis. This allows the maintenance organization to be proactive, not reactive.

5. Maintenance Technician Qualifications and Training

One of the largest problems facing maintenance organizations in the next decade is the skill level of the workforce. Coupled with management's lack of commitment to training and inflexibility of the workforce, this problem makes this category one of the most critical on the grid. Close examination of the organization's attitude in this category is extremely important.

6. Maintenance Information and Improvement Actions

This category deals with the maintenance information system, which is the work order. The work order is the key to planning, scheduling, information gathering, communication, etc. The disciplines surrounding the effective use of the work order system spell success or failure of the maintenance improvement plan.

7. Summation of the Company Maintenance Position

This category was included to help organizations find themselves on the grid. Each stage is really a summation of the proceeding categories. If a company is reactive and has most of the attitudes of an uncertain organization, then it will fail to understand why equipment failures occur. It will then do something like fire the maintenance manager, which accomplishes nothing but adds confusion. When looking at this category, an organization should be careful to avoid elevating itself to the highest stage unless all other categories reflect the same level of commitment.

Stages

The stages of organizational development are listed horizontally across the grid. The five stages are distinct enough to provide an organization the ability to be classified.

1. Uncertainty.

Organizations in this category have no understanding of the value of maintenance to their competitive position. Organizations in this stage blame the maintenance organization for equipment problems. The basic problem is a lack of understanding of maintenance and what its real role in the organization should be. However, here is where the problems arise. Everyone knows how maintenance should be done. Just ask:

- The Production Manager
- The Engineering Manager
- The Operations Manager
- The Purchasing Manager
- The Inventory Manager
- The Facility Manager

The problem is each of these groups understands how maintenance affects their areas, but cannot see the global picture of how maintenance affects the entire organization.

Organizations that are in this stage live for today only and have no concept of what the future holds. As long as they can keep the equipment running today, tomorrow will take care of itself. If you ask them, no managers are going to say they are like this. However, using the various measurement categories, look at what they are doing. Is there a disciplined work order system with effective planning and scheduling? Is there a preventive/predictive maintenance program being utilized effectively? Are the maintenance technicians multi-skilled and cross trained? Organizations believe that they have enough problems for today; let the future take care of itself.

2. Awakening

This stage allows an organization to begin realizing what maintenance can contribute. However, it is not yet convinced. The lack of conviction leads to the lack of commitment. In turn, the lack of commitment leads to the lack of proper funding. The difference between uncertain and awakening organizations is that uncertain doesn't care about what the future holds; awakening does care and is somewhat aware, but doesn't want to commit the resources. The results are the same: neither group does anything.

Organizations in this category will talk about long range plans, predictive maintenance, computerized maintenance systems, and training of the work force; however, they don't ever take any action. The lack of action is caused by the organization's lack of understanding of maintenance and how it relates to investment spending.

A second problem is the lack of understanding by the maintenance managers in the area of advanced maintenance techniques and technologies. I will always remember one management presentation to an organization that used a prodigious amount of rotating equipment. When the presentation turned to predictive maintenance, the maintenance manager said (in front of his executive directors) that vibration analysis was unproved and had no place in their organization. The organization will never understand or commit to advance maintenance techniques and technologies, if the maintenance professionals do not prepare them.

The culture change for maintenance is more evident in the area of computerized maintenance systems. Many organizations in the awakening stage feel that this is a quick fix to their problems. Unfortunately, they fail to realize that this is a project with an average of approximately 10 months of implementation time and a payback of 15 months. This lack of understanding has contributed to many failed improvement programs. Organizations will never move out of awakening category without acquiring a good understanding of maintenance basics.

3. Enlightenment

Organizations moving from awakening to enlightenment do so through education. These organizations come to understand clearly the value of maintenance. They acquire an understanding of the true costs of maintenance. This involves the understanding of the "Total Costs" concept.

The Total Costs concept helps all parts of the organization to communicate. Enhanced communication occurs when everyone understands the financial impact that maintenance decisions have on the bottom line. This understanding leads to considering maintenance as part of the team. Operations, engineering, and maintenance all work together to solve problems. Finger pointing decreases and team work increases.

Management of the enlightened organization recognizes the value of a work force skilled in advanced maintenance technologies and techniques. The management commitment necessary to achieve this level of workforce development begins to convince the unbelievers in the organization. The workforce then no longer feels management is "trying to put one over on them." They feel the commitment and, in turn, respond with their own personal commitment. The organization is making progress.

4. Wisdom

This stage is where an organization realizes the benefits achieved during the stage of enlightenment and works hard to keep the organizational support necessary to make further progress. This stage requires bench marking and progress reports. The quickest way to step back a stage or two is to lose organizational support for the maintenance improvement program.

Organizations in this category do not think they have arrived, because they know that continuous improvement must be made. The comment was once made that "When you think you have arrived, it is time for the organization to replace you with someone who has better vision." This is the attitude of those in the Wisdom stage. The World Class theme of Continuous and Rapid Improvement is the charter of the organization in this stage.

Maintenance organizations in this stage do not get side-tracked. They know that the way they can contribute to a World Class organization is to help achieve the three goals:

1. The highest quality product or service
2. At the lowest possible cost
3. The best on-time delivery

Always looking for ways that maintenance can contribute to reaching these goals becomes their charter.

5. Certainty

Certainty has reached the stage of maintenance management maturity. This will involve World Class programs such as TPM, advanced preventive/predictive technologies, highly trained and efficient workforces, and advanced use of computerized systems. The organizations in this category have also learned another important lesson: If you don't expect maintenance problems, they will not occur. Although this may seem to be unrealistic, those companies who have achieved this stage know it to be true. Organizations who are still in uncertainty think this to be too expensive and too unrealistic a goal.

Using the Grid

The grid is just another tool for an organization to improve maintenance. It accomplishes a basic task by allowing the various parts of an organization to agree on their present status of maintenance. Once the present status is agreed upon, the grid accomplishes a second task: it allows an organization to plan the future, particularly the actions necessary to improve maintenance.

The third task the grid accomplishes is a reflection on the past. Organizations that are making progress merely have to look backward a status or two and remember how things used to be. This is often enough incentive to make them push ahead for the next stage.

Because maintenance is a support function, its status is fluid. Reorganization or a management change may move the status back a stage or two. But by using the same method to make the initial progress — education — these stages can quickly be regained.

The process of maintenance improvement is important to organizations wanting to survive in the competitive world marketplace. It is hoped that the Maintenance Management Maturity Grid can be of some value to your organization in achieving this goal.

After an organization has been through a self-assessment, it is necessary to identify clearly those changes that need to be made and to develop a time-lined improvement program. This understand of the "as-is – to-be" model is crucial when beginning to select a CMMS / EAM system. Without a clear understanding of the underlying business process, the correct functionality required by the organization can never be clearly identified, much less properly configured, implemented, and utilized.

3

CMMS / EAM Systems

In computerizing maintenance, there are certain processes that must be understood and adhered to by the organization. Maintenance planning is one of the most overlooked. Maintenance planning is a fundamental component of any CMMS / EAM system. However, it is also the most diverse feature in all of the commercially available systems. In order to properly understand how a CMMS / EAM system has evolved over time, it would be wise to examine how it allows an organization to plan and schedule maintenance activities.

Maintenance Planning

Management surveys show the average productivity of maintenance employees is between 25 and 35%. This means the typical craftsman has less than 4 hours of productive time per 8 hour day due to poor maintenance management.

Maintenance employees, whether craftsmen or supervisors, readily recognize the symptoms of a lack of maintenance management procedures, with the result that craftsmen are forced to wait, which means they are spending time unproductively.

Some of the most common wastes of productive time include:
- Multiple trips to stores for materials
- Return trips for tools to do the job
- Visits to job site to see what is required
- Parts not in stock, waiting for delivery from vendor
- Incomplete planning, communication
- Poor craft coordination
- Waiting for drawings, engineering
- Looking for supervisor for instructions, questions
- Waiting for next work assignment, the next job

- Insufficient personnel scheduled for job
- Waiting for equipment to be shut down
- Pulled off job because of emergency work

On the average, every time technicians are pulled off a job for any reason, their rate of productivity is disrupted for a minimum of two hours. This is the case whether the reason is listed above or is unique to a particular industry.

To prevent this major loss of productivity, it is necessary to implement some form of job planning function. Planning can accomplished by the supervisor where there are relatively few maintenance workers. If there are more than 12 technicians, planning is best done by separate maintenance planners. Otherwise, the supervisors are forced to process paperwork when they could more profitably spend their time supervising and directing the work of the technicians.

The concept of job planning is to determine what is to be done and how it is to be done. Job planning consists of two main areas: craft skills and materials required for the job. These labor and material requirements may be converted into dollars to give an estimate of the cost of completing the work order.

The importance of planning cannot be over-emphasized. Planning is to maintenance what production control is to production. In production, labor measurement is impossible without knowing how, where, and when the work is to be done. Work measurement in maintenance is impossible unless the how, where, and when questions are answered.

A clear indicator of the importance of planning to a CMMS / EAM system is the Engineer's Digest and AIPE (American Institute of Plant Engineers) survey. According to the survey, of those companies having a maintenance planner, 91% were also computerized. Planners are essential functional positions for CMMS / EAM system success.

Note: The following is a review of some of the basics of maintenance work activities as they relate to planning and scheduling. Although this may not be a high priority for a stand-alone maintenance organization, those who are progressing toward an EAM environment may find it extremely useful to review this material. The reason is standardization. For an EAM system to be fully utilized, the various plant organizations must be similar in how they execute the maintenance business. Otherwise, it becomes difficult to do any comparisons across multiple organizations.

Types of Work to be Planned

Emergency maintenance and critical maintenance (work needed immediately or within 24 hours) is seldom planned. These requests are of short duration and are performed so quickly that there is not time to plan them. These types of work orders should not be considered in the planning functions.

Normal corrective or routine work orders should be the primary consideration of the planning function. These work orders are received and placed in the work backlog. As the work force and materials become available to carry out the work, it is scheduled. Preventive and predictive maintenance work orders are included in this type of work.

The other group of work requests that can be planned are the shutdown, turnaround, or outage (STO) work orders. For this type of work, it is important that the equipment be shut down and overhauled in the shortest possible time. Only by accurately estimating and scheduling these work requests can the shutdown be successful.

How to Plan Maintenance Work

Effective planning requires the planners to be skilled and knowledgeable in the craft area they are planning. Supervisors or top craftsmen will make the best planners. If a second-rate individual is promoted to planner, the results of the planning program will not be satisfactory. Instead of increasing productivity, you may find productivity decreasing.

The planning begins once the work order is approved by management. It is then assigned to planners, who carefully study the job. Planners must then decide the following:

1. The crafts required
2. The time required
3. The materials required
4. If outside help in the form of specialists, contractors, or special rental equipment is required.

When planners are deciding on the required crafts, they must decide not only the number of craftsmen and the number of crafts, but also the skill level of the craftsmen. Where journeymen may be required for one assignment, apprentices may be able to complete other assignments.

The time estimate for the work order is important. If there are no time estimates, you will never know the man-hours of work that is in the craft backlog. Without this information, you can never accurately determine the proper staffing levels for your plant.

The materials required for the work order will determine whether it can be scheduled. If the necessary materials are not available and the work order is scheduled, the craftsmen will lose productivity look for the parts and waiting for the supervisor to find them work that can be performed. It is also necessary to plan the materials so that an accurate estimate of the cost of the work order can be obtained.

The miscellaneous items to be planned are important to proper completion of the work order. If special skills are required (from an outside source) but not obtained, the in-house technicians may not be able to complete the work order with positive results. Also, if special tools or equipment are required, it would be pointless to schedule the work order without it. Trying to get by without the tools to complete the job generally results in lost productivity. Once the work order is planned and scheduled, the planners should be available in case questions arise on procedure or materials for the work order.

Job estimating and scheduling techniques

When planners estimate the labor requirements for the work order, there are a few useful tools they can rely on to make the accurate estimates. The following three methods may be used:

1. Timeslots
2. Universal time standards
3. Time study estimates
4. Estimating jobs

Timeslots

One of the most accurate approaches to maintenance scheduling is timeslots. Manually, it requires calculations to be performed. Some CMMS / EAM systems, discussed later, will automatically calculate the timeslots.

In the timeslot method, work orders are not estimated as an hourly quantity, but as an "A" job, "B" job, "C" job, etc., for the particular craft. For example, an "A" job may be from 0-2 hours, a "B" job from 2-4 hours, depending on the timeslots for the particular shop.

The timeslots may also be defined by "benchmark jobs" with which everyone is familiar. Thus, an "A" job may be "harder than changing contractor tips but easier than changing a movable arm." A "B" job may be "harder than changing a movable arm, but easier than changing a contactor," and so forth.

In estimating maintenance work, especially when it is non-repetitive, it is far easier to "hit" a wide timeslot accurately than a single time value. Timeslots provide the following information:
- Job estimating standards for every job and craft
- Accurate workload estimates for planners

If the planners estimate a job as an "A" job for an electrician, they must then insert the average for the "A" jobs for a given period of time, for the craft they are scheduling. It is not expected that the specific job will take the specific average for the "A" job. However, if there are x number of "A" jobs, it is accurate to estimate there will be that average times x the number of work orders, giving you the total number of hours in the crafts backlog. For example, if A =1.5 hours, and there are ten jobs, then 10 X 1.5 = 15 hours in the craft backlog for the A jobs. The timeslot method allows accurate total workload estimates by craft. It therefore enables accurate workload scheduling.

To be accurate, the timeslot estimates should be re-calculated every week, using the last 20 week's average, for the completed work orders. Although this may result in a lot of manual paperwork, a computerized system can do this automatically.

Universal Time Standards

Universal time standards are a compilation of the average time it takes to perform standard jobs in industry. They are very similar to the auto repair estimate manuals used in garages. They give the average time required to perform standard jobs. Although these are good benchmarks, they can lead to frustration for the supervisors and the craftsmen. Because maintenance is somewhat unique for each plant, the estimates may not be totally accurate for the site. Furthermore, these standards can be used only when the exact conditions from when the estimate was developed are met.

If the universal time standards are used, they should only be used for guides, not exact scheduling. If planners can learn to use them, compensating for variations in types of equipment, tools, or environmental conditions, the standards can be a useful tool. As was true of the timeslots, some computerized systems make use of the universal time standards.

Time Study Standards

If this method is to be used, it will require a comprehensive time-and-motion study to develop the standards. The time study involves the observance of the actual job steps, timing them while performed and noting the job conditions. Although this takes considerable time and effort, the results will be accurate and customized to your installation. However, the cost, training required, and length of implementation time are major drawbacks to beginning the project. It is beyond the scope of this text to deal with the process used to develop these estimates. Most industrial engineering texts will provide the necessary information for developing time and motion studies.

Estimating Jobs

This method is merely the planners estimating how long the job will take. In most cases, it is the "best guess" method. However, if the planners have job experience, it is possible to be accurate the majority of the time. This method is the lowest cost way of establishing standards. It can be used for planning and scheduling and, to some measure, as a yardstick for efficiency.

The disadvantages include depending on the accuracy of the planners. If the planners are working new jobs, ones having no previous estimations or jobs using new methods or tools, then the estimate is just a guess. Also, the estimations can affect the morale of the workers; it is important that they do not use the estimation as a goal. The most damaging disadvantage is that when the planners change job assignments, you lose much of the data that went into planning the work. A documented method of planning is preferred. A CMMS / EAM system can provide an electronic method of storing and re-using past work order plans, thus avoiding knowledge loss when planners change job assignments.

Gross vs. Net Capacity

Another area where problems develop during scheduling is determining the number of hours to schedule for the week. Do you schedule to your gross capacity or your net capacity? The difference between gross capacity and net capacity might best be illustrated by a paycheck. Most paychecks show the gross amount earned for the pay period. However, what you can spend is the net amount, which is what is left after federal income taxes, state income taxes, FICA, and other deductions.

The same is true with maintenance scheduling. You have a gross amount of hours to schedule, which is the number of employees times the number of hours scheduled for the week. You may add to this amount the number of hours worked by outside contractors and scheduled overtime for the workforce.

To arrive at the net capacity, you should subtract from the gross capacity the following:

1. Average emergency work for the week
2. Average preventive hours
3. Average standing work orders

This leaves you with the net capacity of hours to schedule. If you schedule more than this amount, you should not expect to get it done. If you do manage to get the hours completed, it is because you are having lower-than-average hours in one of the three areas above. Scheduling beyond your net capacity is a source of frustration to the supervisors and the technicians. Also, it can lower your credibility with management for promising something you cannot deliver.

Maintenance Work Orders

Before a maintenance organization can begin to computerize, it needs to set up a method of collecting the information, discussed in Chapter 2. The basic system used to enable a maintenance organization to collect and organize this information is the work order. The work request or notification is a form that is used to initiate a request for maintenance work. Once the work request or notification is approved, it becomes the work order. The work order should produce information on the following:

- Maintenance performance
- Maintenance costs
- Equipment history

By using this information carefully, the maintenance organization should be able to issue maintenance budget forecasts allowing the various areas serviced to plan for the necessary maintenance expenditures.

In addition to the preceding objectives, the work order should also be capable of providing the following:

- A method for requesting maintenance services
- A method to record maintenance tasks and their start and completion dates
- A method of identifying the type of work to be performed
- A method of providing detailed instructions for each step of the job to be performed
- A method of authorizing work when the costs will exceed a certain level

- A method of planning and scheduling the work
- A method of assigning the work to the craftsmen
- A method of recording the use of special tools and materials
- A method of recording labor and materials costs
- A method of generating reports that can measure labor and supervision efficiency
- A method of generating reports that allow for cost analysis of all maintenance tasks

Work Order Number

The key to the success of a work order system is the work order number. This number identifies the specific maintenance request. All maintenance charges (labor, materials and other) are identified by this number. To use the work order properly, a number must be assigned to each work request. This is for any work, whether planned, unplanned, emergency, or preventive maintenance.

Planned work is work requested that can be planned, scheduled, and completed without causing delays to the operations. Unplanned work involves work requests that are of short duration and that may be performed by a craftsman while working on another task in the same area. This work may be of a critical nature that could quickly lead to an emergency if corrective action is not taken.

Emergency work requests (also called breakdown orders) are requests for work due to equipment breakdowns or pending breakdowns. There may not be time to fill out a work order before the work is started. However, to make the system work properly, the work request should be filled out at the first opportunity. This will still allow for all related costs to be charged to the work order number.

Preventive maintenance work orders fall into the same class as planned work orders. They should still be recorded separately so that the preventive maintenance (PM) costs can be accurately tracked. Preventive maintenance (PM) tasks are assigned standing or repetitive work order numbers. These numbers will allow the tracking of all charges made to a certain PM task. This tracking will help determine the cost effectiveness of the PM program. Repetitive tasks that are not PM tasks but are performed on a periodic basis should also be assigned standing or repetitive work order numbers. This system will allow the manager to track the work order costs for specific tasks, assuring that excessive time is not spent on certain tasks.

Work Order Forms

Once the numbering system is devised, the work order form must be considered. The maintenance department may choose to use forms that are supplied by certain vendors, or may choose to make up their own forms and have them printed. However the decision is made, the following are points to consider when selecting a work order form.

Work Order Identification

The work order form should be uniquely identified by an individual work order number. The forms may be pre-printed with a sequential number on each form. The form should also provide a means for entering the equipment number (identifying where the work is being performed) for tracking the maintenance costs. For accounting purposes, the report should provide a space for entering an accounting or project number.

In further specifying the work request, the work order should include:
- Priority rating
- The type of work to be performed
- A description of the work requested

In some installations, the priority and type of work are coded. That is, a list of the possible priorities and work types are made up and assigned codes. To keep the records consistent, each work request is then assigned a priority code and a work class code, identifying the importance of the work and the type of work to be performed.

Work Order Scheduling

To allow for proper scheduling of the work request, there should be some space on the work order for supervisors (or, in some installations, planners) to estimate the following necessary to perform the work:
- The man-hours
- The crafts
- The materials

These estimates will assist in proper scheduling of the work order. In figuring costs, there should be some method of entering planned costs by the requester. In some cases, the work order form may need a space for an individual to approve the work request if the total cost is to exceed some predetermined level.

The work order form should also allow for detailed instructions concerning the work order to be entered. These instructions would include the job plan (how to carry out the work request).

Work Order Report Information

The work order form should also allow space for the entry of the actual material and labor charges. These charges can be compared to the estimates, after the completion of the work order, to determine efficiency.

The work order should also allow space to enter the description of the actual work performed. This description, when compared to the work planned, will help rate the efficiency of the planning. Also, in order to shorten the time required in filling out the completed work order, work codes can specify the work that was performed.

Using Work Order Forms

The following scenario is typical in processing a work order.

Step 1

The work order is received by the maintenance department. The work order request is entered on a work order form with a number pre-assigned to it. This number will be the key to the work order's progress through the system. Where multiple copies of the work orders are used, the number should be clearly imprinted on each copy.

Step 2

The individual requesting the work should be identified on the work order.

Step 3

The equipment on which the work is being requested and the reason for the request should be entered on the work order.

Step 4

A detailed, but brief description of the work requested should be entered on the work order. In order to shorten the amount of space required on the form, the above information can be coded. The following are some of the fields that can be coded:

• Authorizer

- Supervisor
- Type of work
- Status
- Equipment

Step 5

The requester assigns the work order a priority, according to the standard procedures for the particular installation.

Step 6

The requester enters the date of the request and the desired completion date. The requester then keeps one copy and forwards any others to the maintenance department.

Step 7

Planners review the work order request.

If they are in agreement with the requester's input, the work order planning will begin. If they are not in agreement, then the requester should be contacted and the necessary changes agreed on.

Step 8

Once authorization is given to perform the work, planners begin to schedule the job. Once they are assured that the labor, parts, materials, and equipment are ready, the work order can be scheduled.

If the work order is not to be scheduled at present, it is placed in the work backlog. The backlog is a master file of all incomplete work orders.

Step 9

When the work order is scheduled, the maintenance supervisor in charge of the work will be given a copy of the work order. The supervisor will arrange any last minute details necessary for the work to begin.

Step 10

The supervisor assigns the craftsmen to the work order. Upon completion of the work order, the craftsmen report the following information:
- Materials used
- Hours worked
- Description of the actual work performed

Step 11

The supervisor verifies the information on the work order and returns it to the maintenance planners.

Step 12

The maintenance planners file the information on the work order. After the necessary information is filed, the work order is filed in the equipment history record.

This flow process is pictured in Figure 3-1.

Utilization of Completed Work Order Information

The information on completed work orders can be used to track maintenance costs for equipment and department expenses. The two main types of expenses that can be tracked are labor charges and material charges.

Labor charges are taken from the work order time charges, as reported by the craftsmen and supervisors. The time charges entered are recorded as expenses against the work order. The time charges can also be used to enter the payroll information for each employee, assuring that all time is accounted for.

Material charges are taken from the material information entered on the work order by the craftsmen or supervisors. The materials from the stores, including specific spares for the equipment, are recorded. Typical information includes the description of the material used, the part number, and the cost information (this may be filled in by supervisors or planners). This information will allow for timely reordering of critical spares. Space may be allocated for recording any special tools or equipment that the work order requires.

How much information that management is going to require will determine the size and detail of the work order form. A successful system will allow management to obtain the information needed to analyze costs by:

- Work order
- Equipment
- Crafts
- Priorities
- Departments

The backlog of work orders can also be used to determine staffing requirements and equipment shutdown periods. Keep in mind that a work

Work Management Process

Work Management Processes Overview

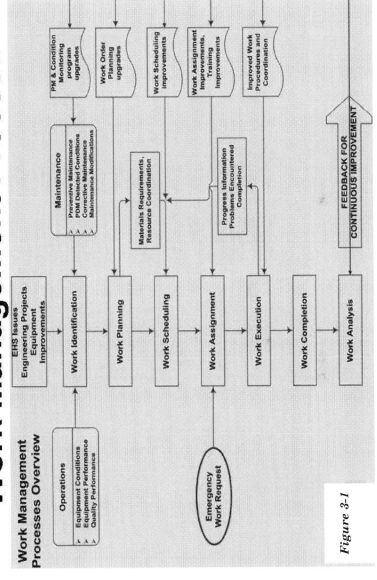

Figure 3-1

order system is only as good as the personnel using it. If the personnel do not enter accurate information or are not trained in the proper use of record keeping, the system will not function properly or efficiently. Through the use of skilled personnel, particularly in the planning and scheduling function, the maintenance department will operate more efficiently. Proper, realistic, and intelligent planning can result in the maintenance work force performing 80–90% scheduled jobs and only 10–20% emergency (breakdown) or fill-in jobs. Proper use of the feedback information available by using a work order system will help management upgrade and streamline the maintenance function as necessary.

Computerization of Manual Systems

Computerization of a maintenance work order system enhances and improves the manual system just described and increases maintenance efficiency, providing that the correct computerized system is selected and utilized. The CMMS / EAM system installation is more effective if there is a manual work order system (or a previous CMMS system) already being used. Again, the CMMS / EAM system is to be used to facilitate the following activities:

1. Maintenance of existing equipment
   A. Reducing equipment downtime
   B. Maximizing the operating life of the equipment

2. Inspection and service of the equipment
   A. Execution of the PM work within the constraints of production schedules

3. Installation of the equipment or major refurbishing

4. Maintenance storekeeping
   A. Minimizing the spare parts inventory

5. Craft administration
   A. Maximizing the productivity of the workforce

In order to achieve these objectives, a maintenance manager requires a substantial amount of timely information. In a manual system, this information must be collected by a group of clerks or supervisors using a variety of reporting media. The volume and the variety of the information is soon enough to overwhelm the staff, and the reporting and analysis processes deteriorate.

A well-designed and developed CMMS / EAM system eliminates the need for most manual paper shuffling and minimizes the information required by any one individual. Also, all the information provided by the computerized system is available to all individuals in the maintenance function, including the manager, supervisor, planner, stores personnel, and accounting.

In larger installations, the CMMS / EAM system is more effective if it is introduced in stages, rather than instituting the entire program at one time. Smaller installations may be able to institute a program without producing an information overload. A small CMMS can be cost effective for departments with as few as five craft employees.

The database required to operate the computerized maintenance management system is developed by input from the maintenance staff. They must identify the equipment to maintain and the parts necessary to maintain them. Because this information is input into the computerized database, it is available to all users of the CMMS / EAM system.

The benefits of computerization include increasing the efficiency of the maintenance department and the production equipment. The four largest cost savings are:
- Increased craft productivity
- Increased equipment uptime
- Reduction in stores inventory
- Reduction in emergency and critical maintenance

The accurate filing and recall abilities of the CMMS / EAM system allows for more accurate estimations of required labor and materials for the maintenance work orders. More accurate planning and scheduling of the work orders result in a reduction of idle time for craft workers. Accurate parts inventory and usage allow for the proper inventory levels for stores materials and the elimination of unnecessary items.

Quick access to the information in the CMMS / EAM system database makes the supervisors of both the maintenance and production areas aware of the progress of certain work orders. With the filing system for work orders in the backlog, all work order trends can be monitored and controlled. Quick access to this information allows for proper staffing levels for each craft to be maintained. The backlog will also help manage the outside maintenance contractors in a cost-effective manner.

Manual records systems make it time consuming to prepare various reports necessary to properly manage a maintenance organization. The CMMS / EAM system, with its almost instantaneous recall, makes report preparation a rapid procedure. The reports from most CMMS/ EAM systems include:

- Use of employees
- Use of stores materials
- Costs for maintenance of equipment

Initially the preventive maintenance schedules are based on manufacturers' recommendations and industry standards. The CMMS / EAM system will automatically schedule the work and the results can be input into the system. Over a period of time, patterns in wear and failures will develop. By monitoring the reports, improved preventive maintenance plans can be formulated. By monitoring equipment costs, over-maintenance, and under-maintenance, both wastes of resources can be eliminated.

Applications of CMMS / EAM Systems

In the previous section, we examined a typical manual work order system. An understanding of that type of system is required before implementation of a CMMS / EAM system will be efficient and effective. With this fundamental knowledge, the application to the computerized system can now be made.

The CMMS / EAM systems basically all function in the same manner. Some will include more detail or use different terminology, but they all will use the work order system. The computer has a major advantage: speed. Where manual systems result in large file cabinets, misplaced data, and communication problems, the CMMS / EAM systems reduce these problems. Even the larger systems require a minimum of paperwork, filing, and time. This section will give a broad overview of a typical system and its uses.

All features included in the computerized maintenance management systems are designed to provide the following advantages to the user:

- Improve maintenance efficiency
- Reduce maintenance costs

- Reduce equipment downtime by scheduling preventive maintenance
- Increase the life of equipment
- Provide historical records to assist in maintenance planning and budgeting
- Provide maintenance reports in a format that is required by the user

Plant and equipment maintenance often comprise a large part of a company's budget. Because of high replacement costs of facilities and equipment, the working life of present equipment must be extended as long as possible. To achieve this goal, equipment maintenance must be accurately scheduled and performed efficiently. Necessary records must be kept. CMMS / EAM systems are used to track all maintenance costs and equipment repairs. This tracking is accomplished by the monitoring of work orders. By monitoring work order costs and utilizing proper scheduling of the work orders, the repair costs can be monitored. This data supplies management with the necessary information to track and plan maintenance budgets.

A second method of cost control is the monitoring of inventory and purchasing. This function tracks the equipment parts costs to each piece of equipment. This function will also help avoid excessive inventories. The purchasing module will help with vendor selection and monitor shipping time.

Another prime feature of the CMMS / EAM system is the scheduling of the preventive maintenance function. Proper scheduling of preventive maintenance can reduce over-maintenance and still increase up-time and extend the life of the facilities and equipment. There are additional costs incurred when the system is installed. However, the total maintenance costs will decrease over a period of time. This overall reduction is shown in Figure 3-2.

Most CMMS / EAM systems accomplish these objectives through the use of four system modules. These four modules are:

1. Work Order Planning and Scheduling
2. Maintenance Stores Controls
3. Preventive Maintenance
4. Maintenance Reports

Each of these functions will be discussed in the following sections.

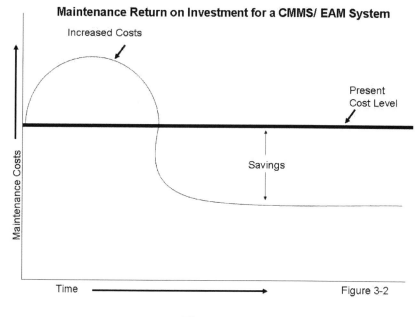

Figure 3-2

Work Order Planning and Scheduling

Computerized work orders are documents that detail maintenance work. They should contain information such as:

- Work order number
- Equipment that work is requested on
- Description of work requested
- Type of work required (emergency, routine, PM, etc.)

As discussed earlier, the individual work orders provide the documentation necessary to:

- control maintenance performance
- control job and plant costs
- track equipment history

The basis for an effective work order system is the same as the manual system — the work order number. All material and labor costs are charged to this number.

Work orders must be input into the system from a maintenance request form, which is filled in by the individual requesting the maintenance work. Once the work order is in the system, the user may look at the work order, update it as it is being worked on, and remove it from the backlog once it has been completed.

The following sections explain the steps used to process work orders in a typical CMMS / EAM system.

Work Order Entry

The first computerized maintenance management function required is the entering and filing of the work order request information. This process has four main objectives:

1. To provide a means of entering and updating work orders
2. To provide the ability to inquire into various parts of a work order
3. To provide a method of charging costs to a work order
4. To provide a method of saving the data on a completed work order

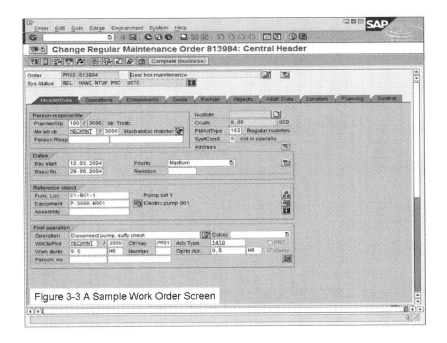

Figure 3-3 A Sample Work Order Screen

Work orders are entered into the system using the work order entry screen. The process is similar to filling out a manual work order. A sample work order screen is pictured in Figure 3-3.

The user should specify the equipment number of the equipment that requires the maintenance. Other information that should be entered include the priority and a description of the work required. There may also be a field for estimating the cost of performing the work order. Some work orders are for complex jobs that will actually require many work orders to be written. When one work order is broken into several smaller work orders for planning and scheduling, these smaller work orders are classified as dependent work orders.

Once a work order is entered into the system, a function is needed for information changes and updates. The information may require changing as the work order becomes defined in more detail. It is possible that more work will be required than previously estimated. Work orders may also require changing if the cost estimates are in error.

There should also be a function allowing users to look at any information on a given work order. This may be combined with the update function or may be a separate function.

Some work orders will be broken into smaller dependent work orders, usually called sub-work orders. This means that the work requested is large or complex in nature, and must be broken down into several steps or phases. In this case, the CMMS / EAM system should allow for the display of the sub-work orders. In most cases, upon entering the master work order number; the sub-work orders are displayed along with a brief description of each. These functions should also display the planned time left for completion.

Work Order Backlog

The backlog is the storage area for all active work orders. As work orders are entered, they are taken by the CMMS / EAM system and placed in the backlog file. The backlog is the computerized database of all active work orders.

All work orders entered into the system will remain in the backlog until they are either canceled or completed. By utilizing the backlog, it is possible to look through all active work orders. The backlog search function should also allow the user to select certain work orders by common criteria or characteristics. These include equipment number, priority, planner, supervisor, work class, safety work order status, and whether or not a shut down is required to work on the work order.

Planning and Scheduling Work Orders

The CMMS / EAM system's functions for work order planning provide the information needed to plan work orders. The work order planning function has four objectives. These are:

    a. Provide an efficient method of requesting and assigning work performed by maintenance personnel.

    b. Provide an efficient method of transmitting written instructions on the work that is required and how it is to be done.

    c. Provide a method of estimating and then recording actual maintenance costs.

    d. Provide a method of gathering the information necessary to prepare reports for management.

All work orders require certain information to insure that the work is carried out properly. The CMMS / EAM system should provide fields for entering the following information during work order planning:

- Labor requirements
- Material requirements
- Tool requirements
- Work order instructions

The individual planning the work order is responsible for entering this information on the work order. When the technicians receive a copy of the work order, the details insure the work is carried out as requested. Planning the work order including details on what work needs to be performed and the required labor, tools, and materials. In order for the work order to be scheduled properly and completed on a timely basis, this information is required.

Crafts

Work orders require different crafts, depending on the type of work to be performed. This screen helps the individuals doing the planning to schedule the proper crafts for the work order. The following information may be entered:

- Craft
- Number of craftsmen
- Planned hours

By using this information, technicians can be scheduled so that the work order is carried out in the most efficient manner.

Work Order Instructions

There are occasions when a work order becomes complicated, and more information is needed than can be written on the work order. This option can be used to add details. The option can also be used if certain individuals are to be notified when the work begins or reaches a certain point. A work order detail with multiple operations is shown in Figure 3-4.

Materials

When a work order requires more than just an inspection, it will also require materials. It is frustrating to craftsmen to begin a job and find that the required parts are not available. The CMMS / EAM system insures that the parts are available before the work order is scheduled. The materials should provide the following information:

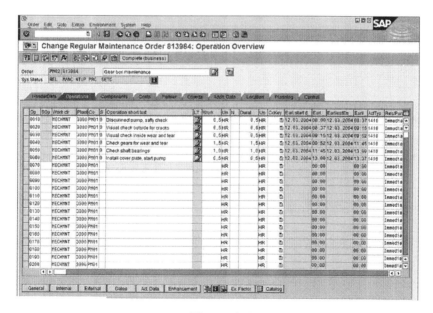

Figure 3-4

- Stock number of required parts
- Quantity required
- Cost per item
- Description of item

There are several ways this can be done. One is the use of an inventory screen or pick list combination. Some pick lists for the inventory may include the option of charging overhead for the materials used.

Tools

When planning the work order, note that some special tools are required to carry out the work. The computerized maintenance management system should allow the individuals doing the planning to note the tools required. The information entered includes the following:

- Tool ID
- Description of the tool
- Quantity required
- Cost (if necessary)

Entering the above information will prevent the craftsmen from beginning a work order without the proper equipment.

Dependencies

When documenting shutdowns, turnarounds, outages, or complex jobs, the work is usually broken down into multiple work orders. Because these types of work activities are performed in a sequence, it is necessary to determine the order of execution of these activities. The order in which the work is performed may require one or more work activities to be started or finished before others can begin. These types of relationship are referred to as dependencies.

When one work order depends on another, the dependencies should be noted. This insures that any necessary work orders have been performed before the next one is scheduled. For example, it would be difficult to install a component before it has been removed and sent out for repair. It is best to use this type of a function if the work order is part of a larger job plan.

Work Order Updates

As conditions change, it is possible that some of the information on the work order plan may require modifying or changing. The computerized maintenance management system should provide that option. The change options should include:

- Crafts
- Work order instructions
- Materials
- Tools

Equipment History Inquiry

The computerized maintenance management system should allow users to look at the history records for any equipment. This information can be used for decisions concerning the equipment.

The records may be accessed all at once or may be broken into three smaller groups. Typical groups are:

- Emergency repair history
- PM history
- Normal repair history

By observing the equipment history, repetitive problems can be identified and possible solutions to the problems recommended. The equipment history inquiry also will help track costs on the equipment. The following costs are samples that could be accumulated:

- Labor
- Material
- Other
- Cumulative

Equipment Parts Catalog Inquiry

The equipment parts catalog inquiry (also referred to as the Bill of Material or BOM inquiry) is an essential function for any individuals performing the planning. This function should display all of the store stock items listed as parts for a piece of equipment. Once the equipment number is keyed in, the following information should be displayed:

- Manufacturers part number
- Part description
- Stock number
- Quantity used on this piece of equipment

Scheduling

Work order scheduling utilizes the work orders that are entered into the backlog. Those individuals doing the scheduling select the work orders to be scheduled. They should be able to select the work orders based on any field of information.

The normal process is to place the work order on a ready-to-schedule listing. This is a list of work orders that are ready to be performed. The individual doing the scheduling will select the work orders to be scheduled for the next schedule period (usually the next week) from the ready-to-schedule listing by the date the work is needed to be performed and by the work priority.

If there are spares in the stores, the CMMS / EAM system notifies users that the spares are available. If the items are not in the stores, the CMMS / EAM system notifies users that the items are not available and need to be ordered.

Some CMMS / EAM systems have a feature that daily checks the stores to see if the short items for the work order have been received. If the material has been received, schedulers are notified by an on-the-screen message.

Weekly Schedules

This feature is used to schedule the work orders for execution by the craftsmen. When placed on the daily schedule, the work order will be printed for distribution.

Work Order Completion

Work order completion allows users to complete the displayed work order and remove the completed work order from the active file. The CMMS / EAM system should allow for the actual hours worked as well as entry of the various material and labor costs that are charged against the work order. There should also be a space to enter any comments that are required. The system then stores this information for use in the historical and report files.

Work Order Cost Charges

This function is used to post costs against the work order that are not included in the normal labor or material costs. These costs are divided into three areas:

- Labor
- Material
- Other

Once the charges are entered into the proper field, the computerized maintenance management system will add the charges to the work order for a complete record of expenses.

Time Reporting

This function is used to charge time spent by an employee on a work order to the work order number. The function should allow the input of the employee's identification information, the appropriate work order numbers, and the employee's hourly rate of pay. This information enables the CMMS / EAM system to keep all labor charges debited to the correct work order.

Stores Controls

The stores control module of CMMS / EAM system is designed to track material costs as they apply to the management function. This module will help to reduce inventory costs and improve stores accountability. The two primary objectives of the stores control modules are:

- Monitor material status
- Manage material sources

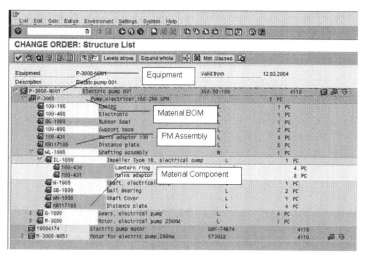

Figure 3-5

The MRO inventory and purchasing function typically begins with establishing a bill of materials (BOM). This is the main listing of a piece of equipment and the components and spare parts that make up the equipment. A typical BOM structure is pictured in Figure 3-5. Additional MRO inventory and purchasing functions are discussed in the following section.

Store Stock Material Issue

This function is used to update:
- Store stock quantity on hand
- Material costs

The stores material, whether planned or unplanned, must be charged to a work order number to track costs properly.

Unplanned Materials

Materials are considered unplanned when a work order has been planned and some materials were overlooked in the planning process. It becomes necessary to issue the materials when the work order is scheduled or even being performed. The CMMS / EAM system should allow for entry of the store item and it should then be charged against the work order number.

Planned Materials

When issuing planned material, the user is releasing the material that was planned for the work order to the employee performing the job.

Stock Return

There are work orders that do not require all of the issued material. When the material is returned to the stores, the system should make it easy to re enter the information. This function should update the stores inventory so that the actual material on hand is accurate.

Store Stock Catalog

To help the user determine if a part is in the store stock, the inquiry feature can be used. This allows the user access to the computerized maintenance management system's listing of store stock items. These catalogs may be used in two different methods. They are:
- Alphabetic listing
- Store stock number

If the user knows the store stock number of the item, it can be entered and the CMMS / EAM system will list the information for that item. If the user doesn't know the stock number, but knows the name of the item, the name can be entered and the CMMS / EAM system will display the required stock information.

Stock Item Work Order Reference

This CMMS / EAM system function is used to show what work orders require specific stock material. The function should list:

- A brief description of the work order
- The amount of material required
- The amount reserved for the work order

To help in ordering the material, the computerized maintenance management system should list the amount of stock on hand, the amount required, and the amount on order. This will allow the user to make logical decisions when placing material orders.

Stock Item: Where Used Inquiry

This CMMS / EAM system feature shows the equipment where each stock item is used. This allows the user to inquire for any stock item to see where it is used.

Store Stock Catalog Index

Each store stock item has a short description. This function allows the user to generate a screen list of all items using the same description. Therefore, the user can access the store catalog without knowing the stock number. The information should include a description, the stock number, and the quantity on hand. This function is useful in searching for items when the stock number is not known.

Store Stock Catalog: Stock Number

This function is useful in finding stock items by either stock number or partial number if only part of the number is known. The function lists all items with the same stock number or partial stock number.

Stores Cycle Counts

In order to insure that the quantity on hand matches the quantity in

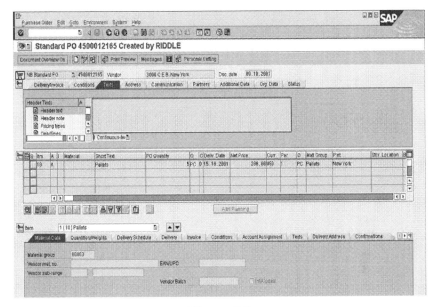

Figure 3-6

the CMMS / EAM system, an inventory cycle count is periodically performed. This is a random manual counting of a selected percentage of the stores inventory. Any differences found should be corrected in the CMMS / EAM system to show the actual quantity on hand. Because only partial amounts of the store stock are counted at any one time, the CMMS / EAM system should allow the user to enter how much of the stock is to be counted.

Stock Item Re-order / Purchase Order Initiation

As the stock amounts of an item are used from the store, it becomes necessary to re-order. This is done by writing a purchase order. The date the order is required by (the delivery date) is important information. This date provides a reference for the user to insure the material is received in a timely manner. A typical purchase order screen is pictured in Figure 3-6.

Purchase Order Inquiry

Once the purchase orders are written, they are entered into the purchase order backlog. CMMS / EAM systems allow the user to look through the outstanding purchase orders. The information should include the amount received and the due date. This allows the user to track partial or late shipments. As purchase order material is received, it is entered into the system. If partial orders are received, it can be noted in the CMMS / EAM system. The purchase order will not be closed out until all material is received.

Purchase Order Update

If changes are to be made in a purchase order after it has been written, they are made through this CMMS / EAM system function.

Purchase Order Material Receipts

When materials are ordered on a purchase order, it is necessary to enter them into the stores stock as they arrive. This function of CMMS / EAM system allows for material additions to the store stock. It should also allow for entering additional information concerning the shipment and the item. This information includes:

- Quantity received
- Whether the shipment was partial or complete
- Where the material will be located in the store

This allows for accurate inventory to be kept in the stores, even when frequent purchase order shipments are received.

Return to Vendor

This function tracks any stock items that are returned to the vendor. This is important for receiving proper credit for returned items.

Preventive Maintenance

This function is used to change or update preventive maintenance scheduling information. A choice is offered to the users — whether the PM is going to be on a calendar schedule or on a schedule determined by meter readings. (Meter readings may be determined by tracking operation time or some other measurable parameter.)

The preventive maintenance module should allow users to define specific tasks and group them by craft for each piece of equipment. The module should allow for entering the detailed information required to do the tasks. This method provides the craftsmen with enough details to satisfactorily complete the task.

The preventive maintenance tasks should be able to be scheduled for day, week, month, quarter, semi-annual, or annual periods. There should also be areas for estimating the time needed to complete the task.

When printed, the PM should allow an area for the detailed instructions and input from the craftsmen. It should also have an area for craftsmen to show completion and for supervisors to accept the work.

PM Meter Reading

This function is used to change the meter reading for a piece of equipment, to keep it current in the computerized maintenance management system.

Predictive Maintenance

Some of the more advanced systems are using the meter-reading part of the system to monitor given parameters on equipment. These parameters include vibration, temperature, spectrographic analysis, and chemical levels. Once these readings exceed a certain level, a PM checksheet is automatically issued, detailing the maintenance action required.

Management Reports

Although it is important for management to understand the computerized maintenance management system operation, they will not use most of the features in the system. However, the maintenance reporting function provides management with the information necessary to operate the maintenance organization at peak efficiency.

Work Order Priority Analysis

This report lists the number of completed work orders during a specified period of time. The work orders are sorted by area and priority. This sorting allows monitoring of work order completions, to insure that the work order priorities are being followed. A sample work order analysis report is shown in Figure 3-7.

Planner Performance

This report monitors planner efficiency. It shows the number of work orders written, number planned, and the planned hours compared to the actual hours it took to complete a work order.

Supervisor Work Order Performance

This report compares the actual hours to perform the work on the

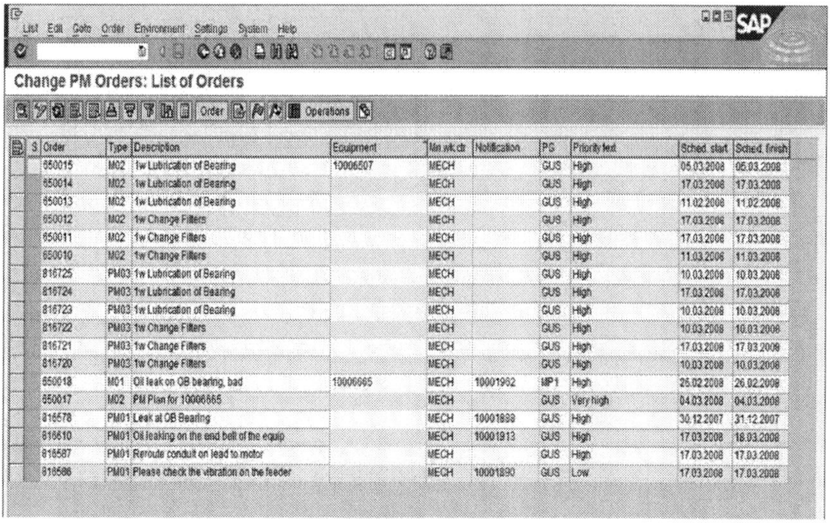

Figure 3-7

work order to the planned hours to complete the work on the work order. This report will be for all work assigned to the specific supervisor and work crew combination. This comparison helps evaluate the efficiency of the supervisor and work crew.

Supervisor/Skill Work Order Performance

This report compares the planned skill hours and the actual skill hours for the completed work orders within the selected dates. This shows the efficiency of the supervisor in managing the different skill groups.

Work Order Costs Report

This report lists the costs accumulated for the various work classes within an area. The report lists the costs charged to:
- Labor
- Materials

Completed Work Order Performance

This report lists the planned and actual figures for the following fields:
- Total labor hours
- Cumulative costs
- Labor hours by crafts

This report allows a manager to evaluate the work order information by individual work orders to find work that was not completed as planned. This report compares the actual labor costs incurred while performing the work to the labor costs that were specified when the work was planned. This report usually requires the manager to specify a start and end date for the time period that the work order performance is being reviewed.

Work Order Backlog Summary

This report provides a listing of all active work orders in the backlog. The work orders are sorted by priority, thereby providing a listing of all work orders that are grouped by what stage they are at in the planning process. This information can support the scheduler when looking for work orders that are ready to schedule. It also will show if there are too many work orders waiting to be planned.

Equipment Repair History

This report lists the equipment repair history for any equipment that has a history. It allows analysis of the information to spot trends or problems with equipment maintenance.

Equipment Maintenance Costs Report

This report lists maintenance costs by equipment number. The costs are formatted in two ways:
- Costs for last 12 months
- Costs for month to date

When this report is selected, all equipment having an equipment maintenance cost history will be printed.

Equipment Maintenance Cost Exception Report

This report lists all equipment (by equipment number) whose costs exceed the monthly estimated budget (also referred to as the cost standard). The report lists the accumulated costs for the last 12 months and the costs to date for the month. It also lists the cost standard for comparison.

Safety Work Order Backlog

This report lists all of the safety work orders in the backlog. The report is grouped by area, planner, and requested completion date. This allows monitoring of the safety work orders in the backlog to insure they are being completed in a timely fashion.

Stock Item Usage Report

This report details the usage of stores material for a given time period. This includes the volume of material used and the total cost. It should also note any items that are at or below the re-order point.

Work Order Waiting Report

This report lists all work orders in the backlog that are not ready to schedule. The report should also list the reason why they are not ready to schedule. This information allows those responsible for the work orders to identify their work orders and take appropriate action.

Preventive Maintenance Overdue Report

This report lists all of the preventive maintenance orders that are past due. This information helps prevent any oversight that might cause unnecessary damage to the equipment.

Report Generator

In many cases information is required that is not gathered by standard system reports. These cases require the use of a custom report writer, which is furnished with most CMMS / EAM systems.

In addition, it is good to consider graphical displays of information. Most CMMS / EAM systems provide this capability. If the capability is not internal to the system, then the data should be able to be exported to an external program such as Excel or Access to produce the graphical displays. This type of display for a maintenance schedule is shown in Figure 3-8.

This chapter covered many of the manual functions performed in a maintenance department. It then compared similar functions in a computerized environment. This information will be useful when considering the development of a CMMS / EAM system specification document in the following chapter.

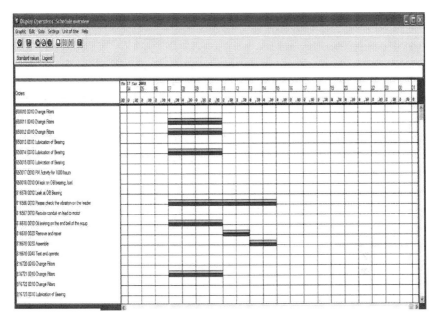

Figure 3-8

4

THE SELECTION PROCESS

Do I Really Need a CMMS / EAM System?

After exploring the difference between a manual system and a computerized system (see Chapter 3), and their advantages and disadvantages, the first question to ask is whether you need the computerized system. There is a three-step process that can be followed to successfully answer that question and others that will result. The steps are:
1. Analysis
2. Selection
3. Implementation (See Chapter 5)

Analysis

Good planning and control of the maintenance function are derived from the efforts of maintenance supervision. They must monitor their work force, see that all necessary records are kept, and ensure that equipment maintenance, including preventive maintenance, is properly scheduled and executed.

However, as the equipment becomes more complex, the industrial facility becomes physically larger, and the number of employees increases, the manager needs help managing all of the maintenance information. Increasing the salary workforce may be a temporary solution, but problems will persist. A CMMS / EAM system can help to shrink the problems and complexity of the plant to a manageable level. How does one decide if a CMMS / EAM system is required?

To start, one should examine the present maintenance system. Some questions to consider:
1. Are the maintenance costs for your installation rising faster than operations costs?

2. How much more are you spending on maintenance than you were five years ago?

3. Do you know what it costs to maintain each piece of equipment?

4. Do your maintenance craftsmen spend most of their time waiting to work?

5. Do you have storage bins full of spare parts that never seem to be used?

6. Does your equipment seem to break down at the worst possible time without any warning?

7. Do you have access to the information needed to properly plan for the future?

8. Is this information in a usable form?

If these questions call attention to problem areas in your facility, it would be wise for you to investigate a CMMS / EAM system. However, if you feel that the maintenance at your facility is satisfactory, consider the fact that a CMMS / EAM system can help to speed up the present activities. Speeding up the maintenance process will not require additional employees. Instead, it will increase the productivity of the present workforce. It also will reduce the time required to search for filed information.

To begin, a study needs to be made of the present maintenance organization. This study will help to determine how efficient the organization is and where improvements can be made. If the organization is found to be efficient, consider how efficient it could be in five or ten years.

It would be beneficial at this time to take the maintenance audit to see how many problem areas are evident.

One additional note: A computerized maintenance management system will not improve a poor record keeping system. Rather, it will complicate it.

CMMS / EAM System Selection

If the decision is made to investigate the computerized maintenance management systems, it is advisable to form a committee. The committee should be made up of individuals from the following areas:

- Engineering

- Maintenance

- Stores

- Accounting

- Information Systems

This committee should accomplish the following:

- Review the present recordkeeping systems and paper work flow.

- Get objectives of the system in the areas of:

  - work order processing,

  - maintenance stores

  - preventive maintenance

  - cost controls

  - required reports (see the next section for further information)

- Identify the type of computer system on which the software is to operate. (If the hardware is to be purchased as well as the soft ware, the decision may be postponed, pending the selection of the software package.)

- Identify the vendor packages that meet the objectives. Some com panies with adequate personnel may investigate the possibility of developing their own software. This decision should be made cautiously. It can be a very time consuming and costly project.

- Evaluate the system and the vendor. This will necessitate contac-t ing the vendor for a meeting where a demonstrating can be arranged. In some cases with smaller systems, the vendor has demonstration programs that can be used to see the system oper- ate. Evaluation of the vendor includes the profile of the vendor, clients presently using the system, and the vendor's support capa- bilities.

- Obtain specific price quotes from each vendor.

This information should then be compiled into a report to manage- ment. This report should provide all the necessary information for the selection of the appropriate system. The committee can include a recommendation if there is a system that is better for the application than any others. However, all the evaluated systems should be included in the report.

The following may be used as a guide to help in the evaluation of a computerized maintenance management system. For a sample of a more detailed specification document, see Appendix A.

CMMS/ EAM System Check Sheet

Rate each item for Importance: 3 (Very Important) to 0 (Not wanted). Compare each vendor you are evaluating to the check sheet. When finished scoring the vendor, total each section. At the end of the check sheet, total all sections. When the check sheets are complete for each vendor, it should provide a quantitative evaluation for each vendor.

Equipment Information

1. Tracks equipment information such as cost center, department, location, etc.

2. Allows for cost and repair information to be accessed at multiple equipment levels such as component sub-component, assembly, sub-assembly, etc.

3. Work orders can be saved to the equipment history as one line of information or full detail.

4. All information in the equipment history can be accessed by sorting on multiple fields of data.

5. The system provides a bill of materials for each piece of equipment.

6. The system provides user-defined screens for storing additional information about equipment items/types, which can also be selected and sorted by reports.-

Total for Section _____

CMMS/ EAM System Check Sheet

Rate for Importance: 3 (Very Important) to 0 (Not wanted)

Preventive Maintenance

1. The system will schedule PMs by the following:

   a. Calendar

   b. Some type of meter reading

   c. Operational parameter (real time)

   d. Combination of any of the above

2. The system allows for unlimited numbers of PMs per piece of equipment

3. The system allows for the following amount of text per PM:

   a. One line

   b. Several lines

   c. Page (s)

   d. Unlimited text

4. The system allows for multiple crafts to be scheduled on any PM

5. The system uses the following type of PM schedule:

   a. Fixed (based on fixed frequency)

   b. Sliding (based on last completion date)

   c. Operational parameter demand (interface)

   d. Operational parameter demand (manual entry)

   e. Combination of the above

6. The system has the ability to schedule PMs for any specific date and/or day of the week.

continued

7. The system has the ability to forecast the following for PMs due for any specified time period:

    a. Labor resources

    b. Material requirements

    c. Special tools

8. The system will schedule PMs for:

    a. Equipment

    b. Facilities

9. The system will combine all PMs that are due for a piece of equipment:

    a. Automatically

    b. Manually

    c. Not at all

10. The system generates the PM work orders:

    a. Daily

    b. Weekly

    c. Monthly

    d. User-defined interval

    e. Other interval

11. If the system does not produce written PM procedures, it provides a procedure code to locate the list of the tasks to be performed.

12. The system produces a report of the following:

    a. Overdue PMs by the amount overdue

    b. Incomplete PMs

    c. Results of PM inspections

Total for Section _____

CMMS/ EAM System Check Sheet

Rate for Importance: 3 (Very Important) to 0 (Not wanted)

Work Orders

1. The system tracks the following information at the individual work order level:

   a. Labor planned

   b. Labor actual

   c. Materials planned

   d. Materials actual

   e. Tools planned

   f. Tools actually used

   g. Contractors

   h. Safety requirements

2. The system produces a report of all work orders which can be sorted by their current status in the work order flow (e.g., waiting on materials, waiting on contractors, ready to schedule, in progress).

3. The system tracks work order backlog:

   a. By craft

   b. By crew

   c. By department

   d. By planner

   e. By supervisor

   f. Any user-defined parameter

continued

4. The system allows work order retrieval from the equipment history to allow for historical job planning.

5. The system will flag any work order planned for equipment still under warranty.

6. The system updates the status of a work order:

   a. Manually

   b. Automatically

7. The system uses the following priority system:

   a. Production assigned

   b. Maintenance assigned

   c. Multiplier, using both maintenance and production

   d. Increased by aging

8. Work order numbers are:

   a. Manually assigned

   b. Automatically assigned

9. When planning a work order, you can access stores, personnel, tools, contractors, etc., without leaving the work order.

10. The system will produce a work order schedule:

    a. Daily

    b. Weekly

    c. Monthly

    d. It does not produce a schedule

11. When the system schedules maintenance work, it:

    a. Lists all work in the backlog

    b. Lists all work in the backlog by craft or crew

    c. Lists the work by priority

    d. Lists the work by date needed

    e. Compares the manpower available by week and balances it against the work load

    f. Compares the manpower available by day and balances it against the work load for each day of the week

Total for Section _____

CMMS/ EAM System Check Sheet

Rate for Importance: 3 (Very Important) to 0 (Not wanted)

MRO Inventory and Procurement

1. The system generates a spares reorder report when the quantity on hand drops below the minimum required.

2. The system tracks the unit price information for the stock items using:

    a. Average   c. Lifo

    b. Fifo   d. Other

3. The system maintains bin location for each stock item.

4. The system maintains on-hand quantity for each bin location.

5. The system has the ability to do multiple warehouses.

6. The system allows for easy transfer from warehouse to warehouse.

7. The inventory system is integrated with the vendors own purchasing system.

8. When the reorder point is reached, a purchase requisition is generated:

    a. Automatically

    b. Manually

    c. Combination

9. The system maintains a vendor file for the spare part to be ordered and the unit price.

continued

10. The system stores _____ vendors per part.

    a. 1

    b. 3

    c. 5

    d. Unlimited

11. When the part is received, the system notifies the planner which work orders can now be filled.

    a. Automatically

    b. By manually searching

    c. Difficult to determine

12. The system produces performance reports for the purchasing section, including:

    a. Overdue POs

    b. Inactive parts

    c. Inventory valuation

13. The system automatically tracks part cost to the work order on an itemized basis.

14. Stores catalogs can be printed by:

    a. Stock number

    b. Part description

    c. Range for either

Total for Section _____

CMMS/ EAM System Check Sheet

Rate for Importance: 3 (Very Important) to 0 (Not wanted)

Management Reporting

1. The system requires reports to be printed:

   a. Daily

   b. Weekly

   c. Monthly

   d. Yearly

   e. Any interval the user chooses

2. The reports produced by the system are:

   a. Just lists of information

   b. Exception reports

   c. Summary reports

3. The standard reports furnished by the system are:

   a. Pre-defined

   b. Created by user specified selection criteria

4. The system allows reports to be:

   a. Printed

   b. Displayed on screen

   c. Stored on disk

   d. Exported to another program

continued

5. The system can sort the equipment history using multiple user-specified criteria to allow for specific analysis of information.

6. The system has a report writer in addition to standard system reports.

7. The report writer was designed to be used by:

    a. System managers

    b. Managers

    c. Maintenance personnel

8. The system has a maintenance budget reporting module.

9. The system reports and forecasts equipment downtime.

10. The system tracks equipment downtime costs.

11. The system allows for searches on partial keys.

Total for Section _____

CMMS/ EAM System Check Sheet

Rate for Importance: 3 (Very Important) to 0 (Not wanted)

Implementation

1. Vendor will perform the following:

    a. Full turn-key implementation

    b. Software implementation

    c. Hardware installation

    d. Data gathering

    e. Data loading

    f. System training

    g. User training

2. The vendor has fully documented installation plans.

3. The vendor will provide at least ten installation references.

4. The vendor has the following personnel on staff (not consultants they use).

    a. Software experts

    b. Maintenance experts

    c. Training experts

continued

5. The vendor's system:

    a. Needs no customization

    b. Requires some customization

    c. Requires extensive customization

6. The software can be installed by in-house personnel.

    a. Yes

    b. No but the vendor doesn't charge to do it

    c. No, and the vendor charges flat rate to do it

    d. No, and the vendor charges hourly rates to do it

Total for Section _____

CMMS/ EAM System Check Sheet

Rate for Importance: 3 (Very Important) to 0 (Not wanted)

Maintenance Software Analysis

1. System is able to be operated by maintenance personnel.

2. System is:
    a. Menu driven
    b. Command driven
    c. May use both

3. The system has the necessary modules to meet our needs (e.g., PMs, equipment, work order, inventory).

4. The system is:
    a. Single user
    b. Semi-multi-user
    c. True multi-user

5. The system is written in:
    a. Cobol
    b. C
    c. A relational database
    d. Proprietary code
    e. Other

6. All system modules are closely integrated. (One posting updates all relevant files or databases.)

continued

7. The system has the ability to archive files and retrieve the files for reports spanning long time periods.

8. The system has a security system that is:

   a. Password protected at a menu level

   b. Password protected at a screen level

   c. Password protected at a field level

   d. Security customized menus for each user

9. The system requires the following hardware:

   a. An IBM PC

   b. An IBM PC-LAN

   c. Mainframe series

   d. An IBM-compatible PC

   e. Other

   f. Is not hardware dependent

10. How long has the product been on the market in its present form?

    a. 1 year

    b. 2 years

    c. 3 years

    d. 4 years

    e. Greater than 5 years

11. When was the last major release of the software?

    a. Less than 1 year

    b. Between 1 and 3 years

    c. Over three years

12. Does the system display analysis information in a graphic format?

   a. Yes

   b. No

13. How is the on-line help available?

   a. Menu level

   b. Screen level

   c. Field level

14. Are the fields edited for correct entry?

   a. All are edited

   b. Over half are edited

   c. Under half are edited

   d. None are edited

15. Has the package been integrated with:

   a. Payroll

   b. Accounts payable

   c. General ledger

   d. MRP or MRP II

   e. An ERP system

16. Are there look-up tables which can be displayed to select entries into the field, which the system will automatically insert into the field?

Total for Section _____

CMMS/ EAM System Check Sheet

Rate for Importance: 3 (Very Important) to 0 (Not wanted)

Vendor Issues

1. Vendor has the following:
    a. A user base of 20 or more sites (all referenceable)
    b. A plan for site visits of similar size and type operations
    c. Two or more years of experience in marketplace
    d. References and testimonials

2. Vendor has on staff:
    a. Programming support
    b. Maintenance support
    c. End-user support
    d. Visionary support

3. Vendor has:
    a. Documented product plans
    b. Programmers to maintain the system code
    c. User group

4. Vendors personnel are compatible with my organization.

5. What is the financial standing of the vendor?
    a. Good
    b. Average
    c. Poor

continued

6. How many systems have been implemented (not sold) in the last 12 months?

    a. Less than 10

    b. Between 10–20

    c. Between 21–30

    d. Between 31–50

    e. Over 50

7. Is there a user hotline and telephone support?

    a. 24 hours a day

    b. Normal business hours

    c. Not available

8. How long is the software warranty?

    a. 30 days

    b. 90 days

    c. 6 months

    d. Greater than 1 year

Total for Section _____

CMMS/ EAM System Check Sheet

Rate for Importance: 3 (Very Important) To 0 (Not wanted)

Summary Worksheet

1. Equipment information

2. Preventive maintenance

3. Work orders

4. MRO inventory and procurement

5. Management reporting

6. Implementation

7. Maintenance software analysis

8. Vendor issues

Total for Section _____

Selection Tips

Although all packages have their place in the marketplace, there are several points that need to be discussed when evaluating them.

Point #1

Be cautious when dealing with consulting firms selling "their" software. This is important because many firms sell the software as a way of getting their consulting services into a facility. Be sure you are aware of what you are buying, the length of any support service, and its price. Some firms will sell the software and charge for a support service that may run for many months. When they charge $800–$1500 per day for this service, the bills can mount up rapidly.

Point #2

Be cautious when dealing with firms that have developed their software for in-house use. Generally, these firms will try to make your organization conform to their software rather than the other way around. They are generally higher priced because the companies are trying to recover their development costs. The support may be minimal and they may lack sufficient personnel to properly oversee and consult during the installation. Also, once the company has recouped its development costs for the system, it may not market it any longer. Be sure the company plans to stay in the computerized maintenance management system arena before purchasing the system.

Point #3

Don't hire someone just to computerize your present manual system. Prepare the necessary paperwork so they understand what you are doing and your maintenance philosophy. If they try to computerize what you have presently, it will not do much to increase your efficiency.

Point #4

Select a system that will grow with you. If you start with a micro-version, be sure the manufacturer makes a mainframe version for eventual upgrading. Also be sure your micro-purchase price can apply (at least partially) to the purchase price of the main frame software.

Point #5

Don't develop your system in-house unless you don't need it for a long time. Most in-house systems will take countless meetings and changes before they become a reality. It is much less expensive to select an off-the-shelf program that closely meets your needs. The only time in-house development should be considered is when no program suits your needs. Given the present number of vendors, this scenario is highly unlikely.

Point #6

Do not select the hardware and then shop for your software. Doing so may restrict your choice of programs. It is best to select the software first; then buy the matching hardware.

Point #7

Price the entire package, not just the software. Many companies add extra costs that do not show up until they are requested. Be sure you understand what you are buying and how much service is included.

Point #8

Thoroughly check the reputation of the vendor with whom you are dealing. There no better method than to call sites where the system is presently in operation. These calls will help you understand the level of satisfaction the customer has with the product. To be fair to yourself and the vendor, check at least three different sites.

Point #9

Understand the difference between each vendor's maintenance agreement and licensing agreement. Some vendors will sell you the package as is, with the option of subscribing to a maintenance fee that provides you with updates and software service support for the year. This feature is not required. They will sell you the software and you do not have to have the ongoing support. Some firms use a licensing agreement that requires you to pay a yearly fee — and there is no option. Be sure you understand the package you are buying. Otherwise, you might face unanticipated costs.

Reviewing the material in this chapter before selecting a CMMS / EAM system can save your company valuable time and resources. The process outlined in this chapter has been utilized for many years, with a high rate of success.

5

THE CMMS/EAM SYSTEM IMPLEMENTATION PROCESS

This phase of purchasing a computerized maintenance management system has much to do with the success or failure of the project. If the implementation process is rushed or left incomplete, the system will not provide satisfactory performance. The implementation can be divided into the following steps:

1. Develop the project plan and resource requirements

2. Update all current records

3. Software installation

4. Data entry / migration

5. System introductions and updates

6. CMMS / EAM system training

1. Develop the Project Plan and Resource Requirements

The activities listed below are those typically required to achieve a successful CMMS / EAM system implementation. The activities are arranged in the sequence in which they should be performed. Certain critical activities must be performed before the CMMS / EAM system can be utilized.

These implementation steps are:

• The task

• A brief description of the task

• Duration of the task

- Manpower required performing the task

These estimates are based on typical-sized sites, with basic maintenance practices and maintenance record keeping in place. Sites with well-established policies and practices in place may take less time. Sites starting from the ground up in any given area will require more resources.

The scope of the implementation project also will determine the required resources. For corporate CMMS / EAM system implementations, it is necessary to form a corporate steering committee for CMMS implementation to insure consistent usage of the system from site to site. In addition, there are some policies and practices that should be applied at each site to insure data integrity once the CMMS is in full use.

A. Establish the Site Implementation Team

The site implementation team should consist of a representative of each of the departments affected by the CMMS / EAM system implementation. At a minimum this would include:

- Maintenance
- Information Systems
- Operations / Production
- Facilities

- Stores / Inventory
- Purchasing
- Engineering
- Plant Management

The team members must be able to commit the time to carry out their assigned tasks in a timely manner. The team leader should be from the maintenance department. This team should be established by the corporate steering committee with input from the various departments as to personnel for the team.

Time Required: 1 day per site

B. Establish Secondary Site Implementation Teams

These secondary site implementation teams are assigned certain ongoing responsibilities. They must act independently of the site project committee (but still report to the committee for coordination of activities) in order to accomplish their objectives in a timely manner. Seven teams are recommended at this time.

1) Communication and Employee Awareness
The charge of this team is to keep all plant personnel informed as

to the progress and purpose of the CMMS / EAM System implementation.

2)   *Equipment and Asset Numbering*
     The charge of this team is to give all equipment and assets a specific identifier. This team should coordinate their efforts with the other sites and with the Information Systems department to insure (a) data consistency and (b) the data format will work with the CMMS / EAM System.

3)   *Storeroom Part Numbering and Data Specification*
     The charge of this team is to insure the numbering scheme is consistent with the CMMS / EAM System corporate scheme and to specify what data must be collected on each item to insure (a) consistency and (b) the data format will work with the CMMS / EAM system.

4)   *Equipment and Asset Format and Specification*
     The charge of this team is to specify the required information for each equipment item and asset. This team also coordinates their efforts with other sites to insure (a) consistency of data and (b) the format works with the CMMS / EAM system.

5)   *Equipment and Asset Preventive Maintenance Program Review*
     The charge of this team is to evaluate the current preventive maintenance program and make recommendations for changes that would (a) improve the effectiveness of the program and (b) insure the program and its format would work with the CMMS / EAM system.

6)   *CMMS/ EAM System Procedure Review*
     The charge of this team is to review all activities at the site that will eventually be performed through the CMMS / EAM System. The team will develop written policies and procedures for each department related to the identified activities. Some typical examples include:
     - How to initiate a work order

     - How to plan a work order

- How to request materials

- How to initiate a purchase order

- How to receive materials

- How to charge time and materials

This team should be made up of representatives from each area affected by the CMMS / EAM system implementation. The representatives must have authority to make policy decisions for their respective departments. This committee may be made up of individuals from the site implementation team.

7) *Training Committee*
   This committee is responsible for defining the training requirements for each of the users. It should be comprised of representatives from each of the organizations involved in the use of the CMMS / EAM system.

Each team member from the above teams should receive training on the CMMS / EAM system prior to the committee beginning any activity. The training requirements for each team member will run from a minimum of two days to a maximum of five days.

C. Resource Commitment by Task

The following information details the approximate resources that are required to accomplish the basic tasks for system implementation. The resources are approximated based on similar-sized sites. Some resources are defined by the number of equipment items, stores items, and general data required by the CMMS / EAM system. (The sample data included is for example purposes only.)

1) Communications and Employee Awareness Program

Time Required: 1 person for 2 hours per week for the length of the implementation

2) Review and Definition of the CMMS / EAM System — Related Procedures and Organizational Adjustments

Time Required: 320 hours (Usually 4 people for 80 hours)

3) Development of the Written CMMS / EAM System — Related Policies and Procedures to Support and Define the Organization Defined in Step B

Time Required: 160 hours (Usually 4 people for 40 hours)

4) Development of the Nameplate Data Formats — Equipment and Stores

Time Required: 80 Hours (Usually 2 people for 40 Hours)

5) Development of Accounting Information Formats — Cost Centers, Account Codes, etc.

Time Required: 40 hours (Usually 1 person)

6) Review of Equipment/Asset Numbers, Descriptions, and Locations

Time Required: 200 hours (Usually 1 person)

7) Development and Review of Employee and Trades Data Formats

Time Required: 40 Hours (Usually 1 person)

8) Development and Review of the Preventive Maintenance Program

Time Required: 12,480 hours (6 people for 1 year)

4492 equipment items X 3 PMs per item = 13,476 PMs

9) Gathering of the Nameplate Date for Equipment and Assets

Time Required: For 4500 items, 4500 hours (should utilize 2–4 people)

10) Gathering of All of the Nameplate Data for Inventory Items

Time Required: For 15,000 items, 15,000 hours (should utilize 2-4 people)

11) Development and Review of All Purchasing Related Date Formats

Time Required: 120 hours (usually 3 people for 40 hours)

12) Assigning Spare Parts to Equipment

Time Required: 960 Hours (usually 2 people for 3 months)

13) Purchasing Data Gathering

Time Required: Unknown

These estimated times can vary depending on the amount and condition of the data currently developed by the site. However, the data integrity must be completely accurate and valid. Any flawed data entered during the system startup will guarantee flawed data later during system use.

This estimate does not include the time and resources required to enter the data once it is all identified and gathered. If the data is gathered in the correct format, the entry time can be reduced by utilizing temporary data entry clerks. It is not recommended that plant personnel be utilized to enter the data into the CMMS / EAM System.

Summary

Project A	14 months X 8 hours	112 hours
Project B	4 People X 80 hours	320 hours
Project C	4 People X 40 hours	160 hours
Project D	2 people X 40 hours	80 hours
Project E	1 person X 40 hours	40 hours
Project F	1 person X 200 hours	200 hours
Project G	1 person X 40 hours	40 hours
Project H	6 people x 2080 hours	12,480 hours
Project I	4 people for 1125 hours	4500 hours
Project J	8 people for 1875 hours	15,000 hours
Project K	3 people for 40 hours	120 hours
Project L	Unknown	
Total Hours Required		33,052 hours

Using this number as an approximation, it would require about 16 people dedicated for a 12-month implementation period. It appears as well that the CMMS / EAM system would require a 12–14 month implementation period. If the resources are constrained, the implementation could easily go over the 16–24 month time period. Implementations over 16 months have a greater failure rate than those in the 12–14 month time period.

This model assumes that good maintenance organizational controls are currently in place, with an auditing system for the maintenance function and a proper level of maintenance supervisors and planners.

With the implementation at CMMS taking this long, the other plants will likely become frustrated at the time they must wait their turn. It might, therefore, be advisable to do parallel implementations, with a large and a small site. One large site could start the process and one of the small sites — which would require fewer resources — could be started within a short time period afterwards. This time period should be 1 month or less. Once the smaller site is up and running, then the next smallest site could be started. When the larger site is finished, the next larger site could be started.

The following list is a sample of the implementation steps. This list of items can be used to start the project descriptions for entering into a project management software product.

Proposed CMMS Implementation Flow Process

1. Establish the corporate steering committee for CMMS / EAM system.

2. Establish the site implementation team.

3. Establish site project teams.

4. Promote Kick-off meeting for site and project teams.

5. Install hardware and the CMMS software.

6. Initialize the CMMS software.

7. Provide initial training for the site and project teams.

8. Define organizational procedures for CMMS use.

9. Develop the written CMMS-related procedures.

10. Restructure the organization, if required.

11. Begin developing various data collection formats.

12. Using the formats defined in step 11, begin the data collection process.

    a. Equipment

    b. Stores

    c. PMs

    d. Personnel

    e. Purchasing

    f. Accounting

13. Begin data entry process (se the same order as in step 12).

14. Begin end user training on the CMMS system.

15. Establish stores stock levels — physical count.

16. Begin using work order system.

17. Monitor all usage of the CMMS system closely for the first week.

    a. Gradually loosen monitoring for the next 30days.

18. Audit the CMMS system usage at the end of 30 days for problems.

19. Continue 30-day audits for the first six months of system use.

2. Update All Current Records

This phase of the implementation can be performed before the system arrives. Although it may seem to be a waste of time and resources, it is imperative for the information to be as factual and up to date as possible. Putting old, inaccurate information will cause all information produced by the system to be inaccurate. In the initial stages, this type of problem would cast doubt on the reliability of the system. You should work with the selected vendor to confirm or develop the format the information is required to be input into the system. This will insure that the information is compiled correctly. Generally, if you are buying a software package, some adjustments will be required.

There are many guides and templates that can be used for data collection. Figures 5-1 through 5-6 highlight the decisions that need to be made just for the equipment that will be entered into the CMMS / EAM system.

Similar decisions will need to be made for each of the classes of major data components that will be entered into the CMMS / EAM sys-

Equipment Identification

- Numbering Schemes
  - Intelligent
  - Meaningful
  - Concise
- Area Location Scheme
  - Divide Plant
  - Area Numbers
- Secondary Type Number
  - Component Type
- Specific Number
  - Identify Individuals

Figure 5-1

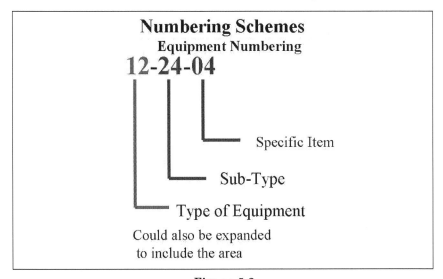

Figure 5-2

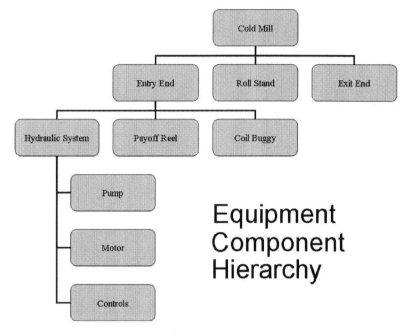

Equipment Component Hierarchy

Figure 5-3

Equipment Location Hierarchy

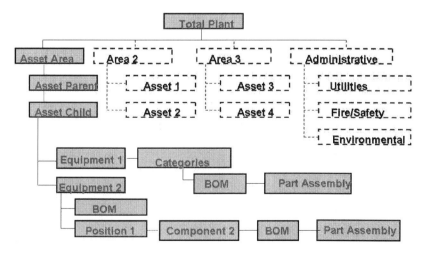

Figure 5-4

Typical Equipment Data

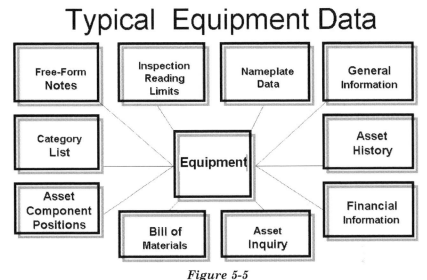

Figure 5-5

tem. For example, Figure 5-1 outlines some of the issues relating to the data for equipment. Figure 5-2 highlights a suggested numbering format that is related to the type of equipment. This format can also be expanded to include area- or department-specific identifiers. Figures 5-3 and 5-4 highlight the difference between an equipment-specific hierarchy and a location-specific hierarchy. These figures demonstrate that there are multiple paths a company can take when setting up numbering and location templates. In some cases the CMMS / EAM software will also determine the hierarchy because some systems will work better with an equipment-focused hierarchy and others with a location-focused hierarchy.

Figure 5-5 highlights the data that can be collected and stored in the equipment database for a large EAM system. Each of the components of the equipment information database can be detailed even further when one looks at the data that is contained in the component. Figure 5-6 highlights a portion of the data that is in just the nameplate component. If this amount of data is multiplied by the number of components in the equipment database, the total amount of data is quite large. This amount of data is possible to input into each of the CMMS / EAM system databases. This is why the estimates for data collection earlier in this chapter are not extreme, but realistic.

NAMEPLATE INFORMATION

- Type of Equipment
  - Motor
  - Pump
  - Gearcase
- Specific Data
  - Frame
  - RPM
  - Manufacturer
  - HP
- Additional Data that may be contained in the equipment manual, drawings, materials, etc.

Figure 5-6

3. Software Installation

This process may be two different steps. If the system is just the software, it will be a matter of loading the programs into the computer system and making sure that they work properly. This step is typically managed by the information systems department. With the software installed, the next step will be to assign identifications and passwords to each of the employees who will be using the system. This assignment is usually in conjunction with assigning them their job roles or user profiles in the system.

Some vendors will provide the necessary support to install the system. It would be advisable to have some in-house personnel working with the vendor so that they have a better understanding of system operation.

4. Data Entry/ Migration

This step takes all of the information in the current record keeping system and enters it into the computer data base. This information will provide the basis for all decision making and reporting functions. If the present system is not up to date, the computerized system won't be either.

The way that the information is entered will also be important. All similar components should be labeled the same, for ease of cataloging data. The more uniform the information, the easier the system will be to use.

Do not underestimate the time it will take to enter all of these files. Large organizations accumulate a tremendous amount of information over several years. This information cannot be entered into the system in one day by one employee!

For sites with limited resources, it has been found that hiring temporary help will be the most economical method for inputting the data.

For organizations that already have the data existing in another system, electronic data migration is another option. This is usually more economical than re-keying all of the data, but is not always a simple process. The amount of data, the size of data fields, and the data field names can all have an impact on the ease of migration. The data should be audited for completeness and accuracy. If the data is not complete, then a manual data collection effort will be required to supplement the electronic migration to insure completeness.

Data accuracy is another issue. If poor or inaccurate data is added to the new CMMS / EAM system database as part of the foundation, any subsequent data report or analysis using the data will also be flawed. If the

---

EQUIPMENT HISTORY

- Types of Work
- Crafts Involved
- Dates of Work
- Dollar Values
    - Labor
    - Materials
    - Contract
- Specific Work Details
- Failure Information

Figure 5-7

old data is inaccurate, in many cases, it is best to start fresh and only use data entered or generated by the new CMMS / EAM system. Figure 5-7 shows some of the data that is typically migrated into the equipment history. As seen, any of the data in these areas that is flawed will created inaccurate reports that many equipment analysis will rely upon.

5. System Introductions and Updates

This step is important to the system's success. If the system is not presented to the users in a positive, upbeat manner, the effectiveness can be reduced. It is important for the groups to accept the computerized maintenance management system as a tool for them to be used. If it is introduced as "big brother," to watch that they do their jobs better, the employees and supervisors may be reluctant to use the system.

If employees and front line supervisors do not cooperate with the system, they can virtually negate any positive effects the system would have. However, if they are convinced that the system will help them do their jobs more efficiently, they can be great contributors to the success of the system.

It is more effective if users are brought into contact with the system in smaller groups. If they can individually see the action of the system, they will gain confidence in the system and its purposes.

6. CMMS / EAM System Training

As with any tool, a CMMS / EAM system is only effective if it is used. Training will insure that the various groups use the system.

Training is often the most overlooked part of the program. The vendor should offer a good training program. Use the training time built into the system price (or if it is an additional cost) to train several key individuals on the operation of the system. Then use these individuals to help train the other users in the plant. If the vendor offers user and training manuals, be sure to obtain a sufficient supply of both.

Do not buy a software package and attempt to get by without training. Even standard database or spreadsheet programs offer advanced training. Merely looking at the computer courses at vocational schools or community colleges will verify this fact. If programs of that nature require training, how much more so will programs that are as advanced and complicated as these? If the training is not taken, you probably will never achieve the maximum benefit from the system.

Also, if the vendor does not offer training and support, you should question the quality of the system and support.

Common Selection and Implementation Problems

Is it possible to do it right the first time when selecting and implementing a CMMS? Many people, including industry experts, say no. But, why is this the case? To understand why companies think they can't do it right the first time, you need to understand the common reasons for selection and implementation failures. A clear understanding of the problems makes the solutions obvious. The most common reasons for failures during the selection and implementation of maintenance management systems are described in what follows as ten problems:

Problem #1. Failure to assess current and future needs

Most companies have three- to five-year strategic plans. These plans include details for manufacturing, product development, equipment procurement, work force sizing, etc. How many three- to five-year plans include maintenance requirements? Even though maintenance is a support organization, it needs to be included in such plans or at least be privy to the contents of such plans. This will allow the maintenance organization to be proactive in making the changes required to provide the necessary support to other parts of the company. Still, most maintenance organizations are reactive, and this attitude is fostered by the mind set of upper management.

Rather than being able to focus on long-term goals, maintenance departments are focusing on short-term, reactive situations. This contributes to many "false starts" or "wrong paths" vis-à-vis maintenance policies or programs. It is analogous to a marathon runner. You do not find many successful runners staring at their feet. Good runners are observant—constantly watching their environment, their competitors, looking for anything that might give them an advantage in the race. Maintenance departments must have a similar mind set. They must understand their current situation but never lose sight of the goal of total competitiveness. This goal begins with providing the highest level of maintenance service at the lowest possible total cost and in a timely manner.

In far too many instances, maintenance managers are either forced to "watch their feet" or willingly do so while pursuing short-term goals, such as the following:

- Starting a preventive maintenance program

- Adding a maintenance technician

- Purchasing a CMMS

- Getting a vibration analyzer

In focusing on the short term, there is no long-range view of how to integrate these projects into a common, focused plan. So, the manager develops a disjointed organization—pulling in many different directions—without understanding that the small programs are only pieces of the whole picture.

In many cases, maintenance managers will purchase a CMMS to generate preventive maintenance inspections, generate work orders, or track inventory. But as they achieve this goal, they want to make progress in other areas. In other words, their needs begin to change. The current CMMS no longer suffices. Is it the fault of the CMMS vendor or the software? The answer is clearly, NEITHER! The vendor and software met the previously identified needs and provided the services they were required to supply.

The true problem is that the maintenance organization was never able to look beyond its current problems to plan for future needs or requirements. This situation will be damaging to the maintenance managers' career and also to their company's competitive position. When companies provide maintenance managers with the information and ability to plan for the long term, this problem will be eliminated.

Problem # 2. Failure to properly document the system requirements or "get user input"

This failure is closely related to Problem #1 in that the requirements for the system must be identified before they can be documented. However, the closer an organization moves toward maintenance maturity or world-class maintenance, the more numerous are the groups that use the information residing in the maintenance system. Consider:

- Does the system provide stores and purchasing with relevant information?

- Does the system provide accounting with relevant information?

- Does the system provide engineering with relevant information?

- Does the system provide upper management with the information it requires?

If the maintenance information system does not provide the data for all the groups in a format and manner that is acceptable, then they will not use the system. If all groups cannot use the system, it impacts the true savings from having maintenance integrated into other parts of the company. The organization will be forced into a "sneaker-net" mode of operation, which is neither responsive nor cost effective. Beyond this part of the problem lies another in the same category—the lack of user input or user consideration in making the decision. For example:

- Who can initiate a work order?

- How many steps does it take?

- Can the technicians look up related information?

- How many keystrokes does it take to plan a work order?

When a system is selected, it should have not only the functionality required to meet the user's needs, but also the ease of use necessary to make it acceptable to the users.

The third, and possibly most insidious, part of this problem concerns who selects the maintenance software. In some cases, it has been:

- The inventory and stores department

- The purchasing department

- The MIS department

- The engineering department

- The quality control department

- The accounting department

Although each of these groups should provide input into the decision, they should not and must not control the decision. The maintenance department must use the system to manage its organization and job responsibilities. If another group selects the software, it will not meet the needs of the maintenance organization. This leads to confusion and lack of competitiveness for the maintenance department. The cost for maintenance to do business will increase, the quality of maintenance work will decrease, and the timeliness of the completion of their work will suffer.

Consider for a moment:

- In how many corporations does the maintenance organization tell the MIS group what computers they can purchase for the company?

- In how many corporations does the maintenance organization tell the accounting department what software system to buy for accounting?

- In how many corporations does the maintenance organization tell engineering how to design or purchase corporate equipment?

- In how many corporations does the maintenance organization tell the purchasing departments what policies and practices to enforce and observe?

The selection of the right maintenance system must be driven by the maintenance organization that is going to use the software. Although the support groups previously mentioned should have input into the decision, they should never make the final decision. To allow this to happen is to ensure problems during the implementation and operation of a CMMS.

Problem #3. Lack of management support

Because a maintenance system crosses many organizational boundaries, management support is critical to the success of a CMMS. Without the management support necessary to enforce certain disciplines that the system requires, the quality of the data produced by the system will be suspect. If the data is questioned, then each decision made based on that data will also be questioned. This situation contributes to a "why do this" attitude and quickly results in "sub-optimization" or failure of the CMMS. For example, if the inventory and purchasing group will not use the maintenance system or at least interface with it, the effectiveness of the implementation will be 50% or less. The reason for this is that a large portion of maintenance costs are stores/purchasing related.

To obtain and keep management support, the benefits of implementing and using a maintenance system must be understood. This involves using key information from the first two problems (discussed previously), such as needs assessment and user participation. However, one more thing must be done to ensure management support: translate the benefits into dollars. "Dollars" is the language spoken at the level where management support must be obtained. Without financial justification, the support necessary to make some parts of the organization work with the maintenance system will never be achieved.

In addition to the initial support, there is the issue of on-going support. This support is especially critical in times of economic downturns because maintenance is one of the first areas in which some companies will make reductions. Companies making temporary cuts during these times sacrifice long-term benefits for relatively short-term gains.

Ongoing support is maintained by periodic benchmarking reports. If a long-range plan was developed (see Problem #1), benchmarking establishes where you are currently compared to where you said you would be. If you are ahead of schedule, document this point. If you are behind schedule, give the reasons why, and document what has been done to solve the problem.

The main thing to do is to communicate. That's just good business practice. This communication requirement highlights the need for maintenance to be managed like a business, just like all other parts of the company. This approach to maintenance alone will notably contribute to maintaining upper management's support.

Problem #4. Failure to conduct a good search of the CMMS marketplace

The CMMS marketplace is large and diversified. With over 200 vendors presently competing in the market, searching the marketplace can be a time-consuming and costly process. How can the process be simplified or at least reduced in complexity?

The first thing to do is to take the requirements that were specified (in Problem #2) and compile them into a reference document. This document should highlight the needs of the company as they relate to maintenance management. This document can then be used to explain to the vendors your requirements for CMMS software. Depending on the complexity of a company's needs, the document can be as simple as a checklist or as complex as a request for proposal. The more complex the requirements are, the fewer the number of vendors that will respond to the document.

Identifying vendors can be as simple as picking up a directory of software vendors provided annually by trade publications. But how can you reduce the number of vendors from which to choose? If the computer hardware is predefined by corporate edict, this can be a limiting factor. If the hardware is specific, the vendors that have software operating on such systems may be few in number. If the hardware is IBM-micro or compatible, then the vendor choice is more extensive. A second method of narrowing the vendor list is to examine their participation in advertising, conferences, and seminars. Usually only successful vendors participate in these activities.

A third method is to consult companies with processes or manufacturing techniques similar to your company's. By finding out which systems they use or which systems they considered during their selection process, your list of potential vendors can be shortened.

A fourth method is to use a consultant. Consultants can be helpful, but they can also be a problem. Some key questions to ask when considering consultants are:

- Do they sell a package themselves?

- Do they have an "arrangement" with one of the vendors?

- Have they selected packages for one or many companies?

- Have they selected packages for companies with processes or manufacturing techniques similar to yours?

Obtaining answers to these questions will help you select a quality consultant for your project.

The bottom line with this problem is to be thorough in examining the market, but don't take too long. You will have a window of opportunity within your company to conduct a successful project. Don't let the window close before you get started.

Problem # 5. Developing an in-house system

Although this problem isn't as widespread as it once was, it still occurs occasionally. The causes for this problem usually fall into three categories:

1. Someone did an incomplete search of the marketplace

2. Someone feels that this would be easy to do

3. An MIS person or a programmer needs job security

The point here is this: of the more than 200 CMMS packages on the market, one should meet the needs of any organization. Developing software in house is expensive. You still must go through the needs assessment, but then you have programming time, you have maintenance's time, you have all the time for the related groups to examine and test, and you also have support and modification time. In some cases, in-house development has cost 10 times more than purchasing a packaged system.

Then comes the issue of ongoing support. Vendors have support personnel, as well as software enhancement programs. A company that does in-house development must staff these positions. What will these costs be? In some companies, they add up to several millions of dollars per year. When these costs are added to the development cost, it quickly shows that in-house development is not a viable option. The important point is that no matter how good in-house development appears, it is never as cost effective or as permanent a solution as purchasing a packaged system.

Problem # 6. Failure to assess the vendor's qualifications

Once the selection process has begun, the vendor and the vendor's software, services, and consultants must be evaluated. In a market as large as the CMMS market, there are vendors of all sizes and qualifications. The challenge to each user is to find the vendor with the software and specific skills required to successfully complete the project. Vendors may be required to provide some of the following services:

- Maintenance consulting

- Software consulting

- Hardware consulting

- Training

- Good documentation

Specifying the software defines which services are going to be required from the vendor. Then, during the selection process, the vendor's capabilities to provide such services can be evaluated. It is also important to determine whether the vendor has these resources as part of its organization or contracts these services out to consultants. If a service is a third-party service, it can develop into a logistical problem. It is always a good business practice to check with previous clients of the software vendor who have used the vendor's services and to find out their level of satisfaction.

Problem # 7. Failure to test the software

This problem is related to the previous one. Just as you check out the vendor and its services, you must check out the software for desired functionality. All too often, companies will purchase software based on what they saw during a demonstration. Then, once they have the software, they find it doesn't do everything exactly as they thought it would.

The best method to use to avoid this problem is to test the software for a specific period of time. Usually, a week or two is sufficient. However, to be fair to the vendor, it is best to have one of its trainers on site during the testing. This insures that you are using the software correctly and not overlooking any of its functionality. Also, expect to pay for the trainer's time while he or she is on site. Again, doing this is only being fair to the vendor.

Also related to this problem is insuring that the right people test the software. It does not do much good for a manager to test the software if that manager is not going to use the software every day. It is best to use the planners, supervisors, stores clerks, etc. These end users will quickly let you know how the software works and whether or not it helps them to do their jobs.

This issue becomes even more important when you are purchasing customized software. Failure to check the customized package against the specified requirements often leads to problems for both users and vendors. This testing will avoid a potential problem as the system is implemented.

Problem # 8. Failure to plan the implementation

Implementing a maintenance system requires resources. These resources may be financial, especially if you are having the vendor or a consultant do it. Otherwise, the resources will consist of the labor required from your staff to implement the system. Implementing the system takes time. It does not happen overnight. During the implementation, it takes labor to gather data and input it into the computer. Failing to realize this, some managers have promised quick implementations and paybacks. When they did not deliver, these managers were dismissed or transferred.

Most of the vendors that have been in the marketplace for any time at all have documented implementation plans. You should ask for copies of the implementation plan for review. By reviewing the implementation plan, you will see how long the implementation should take for an organization of similar size with similar manufacturing processes. This strategy will enable the project to take place within a reasonable implementation time frame and a reliable budget.

Problem #9. Failure to obtain sufficient training and/or documentation

Many companies still purchase software and try to "learn by the manual." This approach is a very costly and time-consuming way to learn the functionality of software. It is best to have the vendor's training personnel train your people. To allow the users to flounder or to let the vendor's programmers train your people will spell sure disaster.

It takes a certain type of person to train someone to use software, and part of the selection process should include the evaluation of the vendor's training personnel. Again, it is a matter of reviewing the training program and personnel with existing clients. Doing this will ensure that the program has produced satisfactory results in the past.

Training and securing the proper documentation often suffer when companies try to reduce the cost of the system implementation. The first areas that companies often consider cutting are the amount of training and the number of sets of documentation they request. Making these cuts will result in poor utilization of the system. Consider for a moment what some of the most popular adult education programs available in evening classes are:

- Effective use of D-Base

- Mastering Symphony

- Easy uses for Lotus 1-2-3

People are willing to spend time and money to master $400 or $500 programs. Therefore, why would a company spend $10,000 or more for software and not train its employees in its use? A company should not really expect to optimize the use of the software without training.

Problem # 10. Failure to estimate time to collect and load data

This problem is related to Problem #8. However, it is enough of a problem to warrant a stand-alone mention. How long does it take to gather and load the equipment, PM, and inventory information into a CMMS? The typical project will require one hour per record. Therefore, if you have 10,000 equipment, inventory, and PM records, it will take about 10,000 hours to load the data. This rate will hold true whether the vendor loads the data or you load the data yourself.

Failure to properly estimate the time or cost to load the data has caused many projects to fail. Just be sure that you are aware of what the total cost and time will be for your project.

Although companies will occasionally encounter other problems, dealing with these ten will help you do it right the first time.

If an organization purchasing a CMMS / EAM system will review these guidelines and follow the suggested work flow, they will save both time and resources when implementing a CMMS / EAM system. Following these steps will also enhance their opportunities to maximize their return on investment in the project.

Utilization of the CMMS/EAM System

When trying to fully utilize a CMMS / EAM system, there are three main areas of focus. They are:

1. Insuring proper staffing

2. Data integrity

3. Evolving to an asset utilization focus

Proper Staffing

In this age of constant internal change for companies, workforce reductions have become commonplace. This is especially true in departments that appear to be overhead- or cost-driven, such as the maintenance and MRO storerooms. These organizations have been asked to do more with less for so long that they may no longer have the resources to perform their job functions properly. For example, in a recent survey conducted by ReliabilityWeb (www.reliabilityweb.com), 17% of the maintenance departments in over 1000 companies no longer have the maintenance resources to keep their equipment in compliance with OSHA and EPA regulations.

Does this mean we have reduced the maintenance workforce to the point that it can no longer keep accurate records as well? Yes. In most organizations, the clerical support necessary to properly add, manipulate, and report on maintenance activities and equipment conditions are gone. They were terminated in organizations that were given the choice to reduce clerical support or the number of technicians in the plant. It was thought that it would be possible for the technicians to enter their own data. However, the number of technicians was eventually reduced to the point where they are only able to complete maintenance in a reactive mode, with little or no focus on planning and scheduling maintenance activities.

131

For an example of how this happens, Figures 6-1 through 6-5 illustrate how an organization progresses through reduction to the point nothing productive is going to be accomplished. Figure 6-1 suggests an organization that was likely robust enough to accomplish all of the goals and objectives for the maintenance department and properly record the information. Figure 6-2 shows an organization that has experienced a layoff, but where the employees are still trying to meet their goals and objectives.

Figure 6-3 highlights an organization that has undergone further cutbacks, and now is in a survival mode. Their sole focus is simply to keep the equipment running. There is virtually no thought given to properly documenting their work activities or trying to improve the equipment conditions.

Figure 6-4 illustrates an organization that has been downsized. (Please see the article in Appendix B: Downsizing or Dumbsizing.) Now the level of first-line supervisors has been removed. The few maintenance employees left in the organization are now self-directed or empowered. This scenario further damages the organization because the quality tech-

Figure 6-1

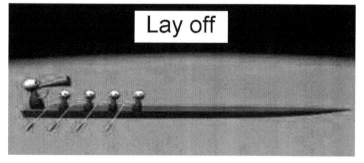

Figure 6-2

nicians will be leaving, seeking employment with companies that will use their craft skills for something other than firefighting.

Figure 6-5 is the final frame. As surely as this person is rowing in circles, there is a whirlpool developing that will eventually pull the company into closing. The only hope for the employees left is that another

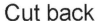
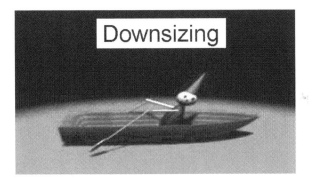

Figure 6-3

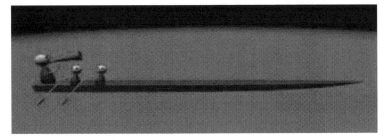

Figure 6-4

Figure 6-5

company will be interested in buying the remaining assets and keeping those people who would like to operate and maintain those assets.

Although this illustration seems beyond the scope of just CMMS / EAM system data integrity, the flow is designed to help organizations to see where they are heading, if they stray too far from Figure 6-1. If your CMMS / EAM system data begins to lack accuracy, which of these figures are you progressing towards?

Data Integrity

Data — information — facts. Whatever you call them, they are important to any manager trying to make good decisions. Producing good, useful data is the goal of any CMMS / EAM system. Even as a CMMS / EAM system is implemented, data collection begins. Consider the various modules used in a comprehensive system:

- Equipment

- Inventory

- Purchasing

- Personnel

- Preventive Maintenance

- Work Order

- Reporting

The basic relationship of these modules is common to most systems and was pictured at the start of the text as Figure 1-1. However, a brief review of the modules will help in understanding why organizations never fully realize their return on investment in their CMMS / EAM system.

The equipment module requires a company to identify each piece of equipment or facility location against which costing and historical repair information will be tracked. The financial information stored in the equipment history is the basis for making repair/replace and other costly equipment decisions. The accuracy of this information is determined by the data provided by the other modules.

The inventory module requires a company to identify the spare parts carried in each stores location. The data required includes (but is by no means limited to):

- Part number

- Part description (short and extended)

- On-hand, reserved, on-order, max-min, etc.

- Locations

- Part costing information

- Historical usage

The data provided by the inventory module is critical to accumulating accurate material costing information for each piece of equipment or facility location.

The purchasing module is included as part of the inventory module. The purpose of this module is to provide the planner a window into the ordering information. Some of the information includes:

- Part number

- Part description

- Part costing information

- Delivery information, including the date

- Related vendor information

- The ability to order non-stock materials

The importance of this module becomes clear when trying to plan a job without knowing when the part will be delivered. It is also important when trying to estimate the job cost without knowing the new part cost.

The personnel module allows a company to track specific information about each employee. Some of the data required includes:

- Employee number

- Employee name and personal information

- Pay rate

- Job skills

- Training history

- Safety history

The data in the personnel module is required to insure that accurate labor costs are posted to the work order and ultimately the equipment history.

The preventive maintenance module allows the company to track all PM-specific costs. The costing information is drawn from the personnel and inventory databases. Some important information stored in the PM module include:

- Type of PM (lubrication, calibration, testing, etc.)

- Frequency required

- Estimated labor costs (from the personnel module)

- Estimated parts costs (from the inventory module)

- Detailed task description

The collection of this data insures accurate service information and costing each time the PM task is performed. The CMMS / EAM system can also project labor and material resource requirements for calendar-based preventive maintenance tasks.

The work order module allows for different types of work orders to be initiated and tracked to completion with the costing and repair information being charged to the correct piece of equipment or facility location. The use of the work order requires information from all other modules of the CMMS / EAM system. Some of the information required on a work order includes:

- Identifying the equipment or facility location where the work is being performed

- Identifying the labor requirements (personnel)

- Identifying the parts requirements (inventory)

- The priority of the work

- The date the work is needed by (NOT ASAP)

- Contractor information

- Detailed instructions

As shown, the work order requires information from all of the CMMS / EAM system modules in order to be truly effective. Without the accurate information, the work order can not collect the required data. Without accurate and complete data, the work order can not post accurate information to the equipment history. Without accurate data in the equipment history, the maintenance manager can not make timely and cost effective decisions.

The reporting module ties all the data gathered by all the modules into meaningful form for analysis. Reports should provide analysis of the data collected, not just lists. Analysis reports should be short and concise, not lengthy and difficult to interpret. The types of reports generated by the CMMS / EAM system determine the ultimate usefulness of the system to the company.

The importance of data collection and analysis to the corporation is highlighted by the following:

- To manage, you must have controls.

- To have control, you must have measurement.

- To have measurement, you must have reporting.

- To have reporting, you must collect data.

The timeliness and accuracy of the data collected by a CMMS / EAM system and its use by the company spells success or failure of the system.

Once a company has purchased a CMMS / EAM system, how long is it before accurate and informative reports can be produced? The answer depends on how long it takes the company to develop accurate data. In a survey conducted by Engineer's Digest and the AFE, the majority of the respondents (over 70%) said that it took them over six months before the CMMS / EAM system was fully operational.

Taking the survey data one step further, over 40% took over one year to make the system fully operational. The information collected by these companies will have some value before the system is completely implemented, but the data will not be completely accurate until the system is fully utilized. For example, if only certain departments are on the CMMS / EAM system (a typical pilot implementation problem), then the data from these departments may be accurate; however, in areas where there is a cross-over or combination with another area or craft, the data may be incomplete or distorted.

As highlighted previously, a CMMS / EAM system is designed to provide a completely integrated data collection system. However, even with mature users, many are not getting complete (and thus accurate) data from their CMMS / EAM system. In the Engineer's Digest / AFE survey mentioned previously, respondents were asked about their usage of the inventory, purchasing, and personnel modules of their systems. One question showed that the majority of the respondents are using less than 70% of their system. A second question broke this data into modules with the following results:

- Inventory: 52% use the CMMS / EAM inventory system

- Purchasing: 32% use the CMMS / EAM purchasing system

- Personnel: 35% use the CMMS / EAM system personnel system

Because the CMMS / EAM system modules are not being used for these functions, what is being used? Some companies are using other corporate systems, but over 1/4 of the respondents are not using any method to collect this information. Even when other corporate systems are being used, is the data accurately being posted in the equipment history? In the majority of the cases, the posted data is not accurate (or not even posted). Therefore, the equipment history is incomplete or inaccurate.

Illustrating this, consider your local garage. When you take your car in for repairs, the service manager gives you an estimate of the time and cost of the job (work order planning). You accept the estimate and the work is scheduled and started. When the job is completed, you are given a shop order with a complete breakdown of each part used and its related cost. The bill (work order) also shows the number of hours the mechanic worked and his hourly rate. The total is then the sum of the labor and parts. You expect this bill each time you go to the garage for any work. If you were given a bill with only the final price, with no breakdown, you would not accept it!

Does your CMMS / EAM system reporting give you accurate costing breakdowns for your equipment? For example, when using a CMMS / EAM system, if the inventory information is not closely integrated, the planner can not be assured of the accuracy of the stores information if it is only updated once per day or once per week. This situation arises many times when other corporate systems are "interfaced" to a CMMS / EAM system. Hours could be wasted looking for a part that is supposed to be in the stores, when in fact the part was used the previous day or shift. Although this delay seems inconsequential, when downtime costs range from \$1,000–\$100,000 per hour, these types of delays may mean the difference between profit and loss for the entire company.

When it becomes time to consider replacing your car, do you look only at the labor charges you have made against it for its life? Do you look only at the parts you used? No! You consider the whole picture—labor, materials, its present condition, etc.

It is essential that these same principles carry over in the asset management programs at our companies! Yet companies have set the CMMS / EAM system information flow so that the material costs or labor costs are not shown on the work order or equipment history. Any decisions they make will be based on inaccurate or incomplete data, and there will be mistakes. The financial implications of these decisions could spell disaster for a company by placing it in a condition where it can not compete with another company that is making full and effective use of a CMMS / EAM system and obtaining the subsequent cost benefits.

The solution to CMMS / EAM system installations where the data is not being properly collected is to reevaluate the current use of the system. What data is being collected accurately? What data is incomplete or missing? What parts of the CMMS / EAM system are we not using correctly or not at all?

Only by evaluating the answers to these questions, and then working to provide accurate data collection, will the CMMS / EAM system usage be beneficial to the bottom line. In the competitive marketplace that every company currently finds itself, it is unacceptable to make guesses when data can be provided. The cost benefits obtained by making correct decisions will help to make a company more competitive. Wrong decisions could put a company out of business by taking them out of a competitive position.

What reports should a company utilize within a CMMS / EAM system? Some systems are available with no reports, whereas others have hundreds of "canned" reports. The deciding factor on the use of reports is to utilize the reports you need to manage your maintenance function. If the report does not support or verify an indicator you utilize to manage maintenance, it is not beneficial, but instead burdensome. Reports that produce hundreds of pages of data that are never used are worse than useless. They can overload the already busy maintenance manager. If you measure maintenance by the estimated versus actual budget and the CMMS / EAM system cannot produce a budget report, then it is not supporting your organization. With CMMS / EAM system reports, too many are just as bad as too few.

Because management requires measurement and measurement requires data, each company must fully utilize their CMMS / EAM system to obtain this data.

- Without data, it is only someone's opinion.

- Discussions require factual data.

- Arguments occur when emotions and opinions are involved.

At your company, do you have discussions or arguments? The answer to that question may mean the difference between being a World Class competitor and being a second-rate company.

Following the guidelines provided in this section will help management fully utilize a CMMS / EAM system.

System selection should be a well-researched and logical decision. Purchasing a system that provides the needs and not the wants will help make the selection cost effective. By not purchasing an expensive system that is beyond the requirements of the installation, the computerized maintenance management system costs can be easier to justify.

Implementation should be a smooth and logical procedure. Proper preparation and training will contribute to an effective installation.

The CMMS / EAM systems will become standards at all progressive installations in the future. Management will have to decide if it is time for their facility to invest in this useful tool.

Asset Utilization

What is asset utilization? It is a new, innovative, competitive benchmark for world-class companies (see Harvard Business Review, May 6, 1992). The benchmark ensures that a company—whether it is an institution, a process industry, or a manufacturer of discreet items—optimizes the capital investments it currently owns. This changes the focus from costs, such as in maintenance labor and materials, to production output. It is changing an organization's focus from costs to revenue. This approach makes full use of the asset information contained in the CMMS / EAM system. How does this transition occur?

Consider a company with a press that has problems with downtime (approximately 20%), can only operate at 80% of design speed (due to wear or some uncorrected equipment defects), and has a first-pass quality of only 90% (with the rest being scrap or reworkable off-spec product)? How close to full asset productivity is this company's press? It would be approximately two-thirds utilized.

In this example, the company needs three presses to produce what two presses should be able to produce. In addition to the increased capital expenditures for the press, what other parts of the company does this mode of operation impact? Consider:

- More operators to run the equipment

- More maintenance personnel to care for the equipment

- Increased investment for spare parts

- More staff to support the increased equipment and personnel demands

- Increased utility costs

This scenario doesn't matter if a company has excess presses and other equipment, oversized facilities, or underutilized processes. When a company is striving to be competitive in its marketplace, can it ignore asset utilization and the resultant cost benefits? Although it is true that companies can produce short-term results by reducing headcount, re-engineering, or downsizing, these techniques do not guarantee long-term competitiveness.

In this example, it becomes clear how closely related asset productivity is to an existing benchmark currently used by competitive companies: overall equipment effectiveness (OEE). A world-class benchmark for OEE is 85% or greater. Yet only a small number of companies actually calculate an asset productivity indicator, and even fewer achieve world-class results. For lack of any other benchmark or indicator, companies cut costs in a short-term, reactive mode. This may help short-term survival while creating long-term problems. It is only by investigating its asset productivity and performing some root-cause analysis that a company discovers competitive solutions to its productivity problems. These solutions typically cross organizational boundaries, requiring all employees using company assets to focus on implementing the solutions.

The question each company must answer is, "Will we focus on short-term cost cutting or pursue an alternative—making our assets more productive?"

If these three areas are addressed, then an organization can achieve full utilization of their CMMS / EAM system. This utilization will allow a company to fully achieve their return on investment in the CMMS/ EAM system project.

7

CMMS/EAM System Optimization

As time continues on, we are flooded with new sets of acronyms and abbreviations that designate little more than old strategies renamed. These acronyms seem to be point solutions that do not allow the optimization of the maintenance business function, including the CMMS / EAM system.

Currently, the enterprise asset management (EAM) community is swimming in a new alphabet soup, a new collection of acronyms and abbreviations — MROI (maintenance return on investment), TEAM (total enterprise asset management), e-comm (electronic commerce), CW (collaborative workplace), CAM (collaborative asset management), etc. Unfortunately, the soup appears to be the result of using new letters in old recipes. It appears to fit a trend of "when something doesn't work, rename it, and try it again." Each of these relabeled attempts take resources that should be utilized in optimizing the CMMS / EAM system.

This trend is nothing new. EAM practitioners have seen similar attempts with CMMS, PDM, RCM, TPM, and so on. An AMR Research Report for Oct. 6, 2000, states that only 10% of companies have optimized their asset performance. The real question is: "Why haven't companies been successful with improvement initiatives that, on paper, appear to be strategically valuable?

Once convinced of their value, many companies have undertaken strategic initiatives, but the results fall far short of projections. Why do companies fall short of expectations when implementing World Class or Best Practices strategies, which include fully realizing their investment in their CMMS / EAM system?

When the failures are closely analyzed, the root cause usually falls into one of two main categories:

1. Lack of understanding of a strategy
2. Lack of measurable or quantifiable results.
3. No customer service focus

143

EAM — A Review

A brief review of an EAM strategy will highlight how common improvement strategies fall victim to not being understood or quantified. This discussion centers on an enhanced understanding of enterprise asset management. The December 1998 issue of Engineer's Digest ("What is EAM anyway?" p. 56) described EAM as a move beyond maintenance management. The author wrote, "EAM systems seek to manage a company's assets to optimize their use, thereby maximizing the return on investment in the assets. EAM includes using in-process information in a 'health analysis' designed to deliver just-in-time maintenance with production impact included in the optimization equation. In other words, EAM takes a process- or asset-centric view of the enterprise, as opposed to a product-centric view." This view places a high value on the data collected by the CMMS/ EAM system.

In analyzing this description, consider first the concept of managing a company's assets to optimize their use. Do companies today focus all of their attention on getting the most out of their assets, or do they focus on what is best individually for departments, e.g., operations, engineering, or even maintenance?

Consider also the idea of maximizing the return on investments in the assets. Do companies really consider the value of an asset in context of its output, or do they depreciate it in scale with some financial algorithm and discard the asset when they feel it is "used up," even if it is still capable of producing a product in a cost-efficient manner?

Finally, think about just-in-time maintenance, with production impact included in the optimization equation. Do companies focus on what is best for the asset, or do they focus on what is most convenient for operations or maintenance?

If companies are truly going to implement EAM, are they willing to change the way they do business to focus on achieving maximum return on investment in their assets? This issue closely relates to the first root cause mentioned earlier — lack of understanding of the strategy. In this case, it's a lack of understanding of what EAM involves.

In developing the Maintenance Management Strategy Series, the pyramid on the front cover was created. Without reviewing the entire introduction in Chapter 1, the blocks are arranged in a certain order. Figure 7-1 reinforces this point. The arrangement is intended to illustrate that EAM is progressive, with subsequent layers built on existing, already functioning layers. For example, the enhanced pyramid shows preventive maintenance as a solid foundation on which to build an EAM strategy.

THE MAINTENANCE MANAGEMENT PYRAMID

Figure 7-1

Root Cause #1: Lack of Understanding of the Strategy

Studies have repeatedly shown that a majority of companies are dissatisfied with their PM programs. In several surveys, the satisfaction was judged by whether or not 80% or more of the maintenance resources could be deployed in a planned and scheduled mode on a weekly basis. If a company is deploying more than 20% of their maintenance resources in a fire fighting mode, how can it effectively plan and schedule resources? How can a disciplined stores and purchasing system be employed? Without an effective PM program, how can assets be reliable? These are, of course, rhetorical questions. Nevertheless, companies continue to focus on other strategies while neglecting their PM programs. The sub-optimized PM programs then negatively impact other initiatives. The bottom line is this: if the PM program is not successful, all other strategic initiatives will take longer to implement and will fail to produce the desired results.

Also consider also computerized maintenance management systems. Repeatedly, for the past 20 years, studies have shown that companies use only a fraction of the capabilities of their systems. If, as the AMR

Research report of Oct. 6, 2000, indicates, companies are only using about 30% of the capabilities of the systems designed to manage their maintenance, does that mean they are only managing 30% of their maintenance organization? What about the other 70%? How can anyone even imagine managing a business function in which only 30% of it is fully controlled? To do so is to exhibit a lack of understanding of a CMMS strategy.

Consider another common initiative of many companies — reliability-centered maintenance or RCM. It relies heavily on theoretical and historical equipment (asset) data. If a company does not have accurate historical data about its equipment, how effective can its RCM program be? How can root-cause analyses of failures be conducted if only 30% of failures are recorded? What meaningful results will the program produce? Again, these are rhetorical questions. Accurate equipment data originate in and come from a fully-utilized CMMS. So when RCM is described as a failure, what failed is probably not the strategy. More often than not, the company didn't understand what was involved in implementing the strategy.

Another common initiative is Total Productive Maintenance or TPM. It focuses on optimizing the use of assets. Here too, most companies fail to achieve the benefits that should be derived from the strategy. Some TPM programs focus only on clean equipment. What results can be quantified from clean equipment? What financial impact does clean equipment have for the company? I first raised such questions in the May 1998 issue of Engineer's Digest ("Clean equipment won't sell TPM to management," p. 26). The point of that article was to show that unless financial benefits are quantified, a TPM program will not be successful in the long term. Nevertheless, most TPM programs produce few, if any, financially quantifiable results.

In any particular company, any strategy represented by a block on the pyramid might fail because of one of the two root causes pinpointed earlier. Still, we see companies that are successful with some strategic initiatives. Unfortunately, of the 300,000 commercial, industrial, and institutional organizations in North America, only a small fraction (10% or less) ever have demonstrable, positive results.

If you look at companies that are successful, you will discover some common elements in all of them. Following are some points from an analysis of the "Best of the Best" maintenance organizations (published in Sky magazine):

1. The best "simply do the basics very well."
2. The best also take a proactive approach to the management of maintenance.

How many companies focus on the basics? How many companies lose focus by concentrating on implementing some nebulous program that is impossible for their employees to understand, let alone execute successfully?

Again, studies have shown that 50% or more of all equipment failures are due to neglect of the basics of maintenance. Companies will never be proactive without consistently focusing on the basics.

Regarding management of maintenance, how many companies focus on the proactive side? Is it not true that the majority of companies manage maintenance reactively? Is it not also true that most maintenance departments get their performances rated relative to whether they are over budget at the end of the month?

Unless companies take the time to educate themselves about each strategic initiative they undertake — whether RCM, CMMS, PDM, or TPM — they will be doomed to failure.

Root Cause #2: Lack of Measurable or Quantifiable Results

Measurable financial indicators drive executive managers. Whether measured by return on net assets, return on fixed assets, stock price, shareholder value, some other indicator, or a combination of indicators, their performance is judged in financial terms. This measurement system, in turn, drives how their organizations are managed.

Unless departments within a company can link to a financial measurement system, their performance will not be measured correctly. For example, if a financial measure looks at whether a department remained on budget for a month, the practice can lead to reactive management.

That would be the case if a department is over budget one month, and its manager cuts back the next month to make up for the overage. However, the effects of that decision are best evaluated in terms of the impact on the performance of the company's assets. The decrease in performance of a company's assets will have a direct impact on the cost to produce, which will impact the return on net assets, profits, stock price, and shareholder value. Again, these are all indicators that the executive management team uses to measure performance. Unless the link is made between poor asset performance and these indicators, improvement in asset management policies and practices will not occur. It becomes imperative for companies to recognize the link between corporate financial performance and departmental financial performance.

In the past, maintenance (asset) management has been a cost control effort. Headcount, spare parts, contractors, and other costs were given the primary focus. In most cases, the impact costs of maintenance went unrecognized. For example, what is the cost of an hour of lost production when an asset is unavailable? The cost might be $1,000, $10,000, $100,000, or even more per hour. Each such loss has a direct impact on a company's profits that far exceeds traditional maintenance costs. It is this type of financial focus that makes RCM programs effective for successful organizations.

Be aware that examining the efficiency of equipment can also uncover hidden opportunities. Often, due to past practice or high turnover in a department, the design-performance of equipment is lost or becomes dramatically reduced. There are assets that are so underused in some companies that three or four assets do the work of one properly maintained and operated asset. This loss is compounded by the fact that companies often will purchase additional assets to cover the production demand. This practice has a double impact on financial indicators such as return on net assets. It lowers profits and increases the value of the asset base. It is TPM's focus on equipment efficiency that makes successful TPM efforts successful. Unless equipment efficiency is recognized, measured, and linked to financial measures, TPM will fail.

In reality, every maintenance or asset management effort must be linked to a company's financial interests. It doesn't matter if it is PM, CMMS, RCM, or TPM. Without the link, incremental benefits may be achieved, but they will not be sustainable as a long-term strategy.

If companies take the time to properly educate their key personnel about each strategic initiative they are undertaking and link the strategy to financial benefits for the company, we will hear about more EAM successes. Analysts who cover the EAM marketplace recognize this point. Will you help educate the people in your company so that your EAM initiative can be successful?

Root Cause # 3: No Customer Service Focus

When one tries to identify internal customers for each department within a company, the question often arises, "Who are the customers of the maintenance group?" Typically, the answer is "the production department" or "operations" or, perhaps, "the facilities group." Is any one of these a correct answer? Only partially. Each department, whether engineering, purchasing, maintenance, or even operations (who has sales as a customer) all have internal customers. However, in a desire to satisfy the internal customer in an organization, the true customer is often over-looked.

In order to understand the true customer, it might be worthwhile to occasionally review a copy of the Wall Street Journal. The Journal often lists the acquisitions and divestitures that companies make. When describing one of these transactions, the articles always include the words, "The assets are valued at…." If the assets are what are being sold, who has an interest in the value of the assets? The ultimate answer is the shareholders of the company that is either buying or selling the assets. The selling company wants the most money it can get for its assets. The purchasing company wants assets in good shape, assets ready as quickly as possible to begin producing a product or providing a service.

If the assets are to bring true value in the marketplace, they must be in good condition. Who is responsible for keeping the assets in good condition? It's the maintenance department. So, following this line of reasoning, the ultimate customers of the maintenance department are the shareholders of the company. If the maintenance department does not properly maintain the assets, the capital equipment—one source of the value of the shareholders' stock—deteriorates. Because few shareholders ever visit the companies in which they own stock, they don't know when the value of their investments is decreasing.

In many companies, it is common practice to have disposable equipment. That is, improperly maintained equipment that loses value quickly—according to some studies, up to 30% faster. Then, the company replaces it through new capital investments. Is this practice fair to the shareholders? Moneys that could have been used to increase dividends or to invest in other projects go instead to unnecessary capital investments.

This kind of waste happens in many American companies when control of maintenance and engineering budgets falls to managers with no experience on a factory floor or in facilities management activities. Those managers, therefore, make decisions without considering their companies' capital investment dollars.

Unfortunately, shareholders seldom see this kind of management in action. If shareholders ever find out how managers "cheat" them, perhaps they will replace them with managers who will exercise proper fiscal responsibility. Maybe, for the good of American industry, these kinds of managerial changes will happen before it is too late, before we destroy our competitive position in the world market.

When it comes to CMMS / EAM system optimization, it is clear that the problem lies in organizational focus and execution, not in the software. During the past 30 years, the software, for the most part, has been sufficient to achieve the necessary business results. However, the organizational focus to properly utilize and then optimize the software has been lacking. As this chapter has discussed, if the organizations implementing and utilizing CMMS / EAM system software had the correct business focus, the systems could be optimized. Without a proper business focus, CMMS / EAM system optimization will be an elusive goal.

Return on Investment

With the focus on maintenance as a business, executives will be focused on the return on investment for the CMMS / EAM system. Adhering to the following methodology will provide the financial information necessary to calculate the return on investment.

Introduction

In beginning any financial discussion, it is necessary to start at a high level. One of the measures that senior executives are interested in tracking is return on assets. Simply stated, return on assets measures the company profits divided by the total asset valuation. This calculation is actually used by many Wall Street executives when examining the financial stability of the company. Higher return-on-asset numbers indicate more profitable, well-managed, and stable companies. However, because we're talking about maintenance and reliability, how do they impact the return on asset calculation?

The relationship of maintenance and reliability to company profitability is highlighted in Figure 8-1. If we focus on increasing profits in the middle of the diagram, we see that there are two paths to this goal. One is by reducing expenditures, and the other is by increasing revenue.

Decreasing expenditures is familiar to most maintenance and reliability departments. The key areas of expense controls are the maintenance labor, maintenance materials, and good maintenance contract controls. A related expense control is the company's energy consumption. Because expense dollars not spent become profit dollars, controlling expenditures is an important part of increasing profitability. However, this cannot be the only pathway. Clearly, if company expenditures are reduced to zero, the company will go out of business. So there needs to be another focus on how to increase profits.

The second path is by increasing revenue. Revenue can be increased by increasing capacity while maintaining fixed costs. Because

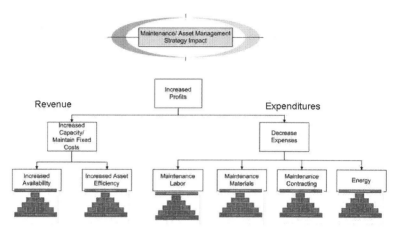

Figure 8-1

the company has already made the investment in the assets, increasing the availability and the efficiency of the assets while controlling fixed costs will also increase profitability. This path has a very positive effect on increasing return on assets. This is true particularly in markets with demand, where all products made can be sold. It also has an impact in markets where there is a cap on demand. In this case, the increase in efficiency and effectiveness will lower the fixed costs.

This relationship is shown in Figure 8-2. If an organization is maintenance focused, it still can contribute to profitability by controlling expenses. However, a larger impact can be made if an organization makes its focus on equipment uptime. In fact, the contribution to profitability can grow by up to four times if an organization focuses on equipment availability or uptime versus just focusing on controlling maintenance costs.

As Figure 8-2 indicates, there is an even larger potential if an organization takes an EAM focus. This focus concentrates on maximizing the efficiency of the equipment. Studies have shown that the largest losses in modern equipment are more in efficiency than in equipment availability. The EAM focus can add to profitability eight times or more than the focus just on maintenance costs. Comparing Figure 8-1 to Figure 8-2 shows clearly that the tremendous financial impact on a company's profitability by the maintenance and reliability department. If an organization can take the proper focus, maintenance and reliability can be a business function, leading to increased competitiveness.

In review, focusing on maintenance controls, along with mainte-

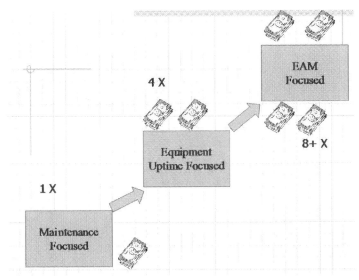

Figure 8-2

nance and reliability expenses, drives out waste, which is the premise of
a lean operation. The next step in the evolution is to focus on equipment
uptime or availability. This increases the capacity of the company. As a
result, the company can do more with the same resources or the same with
fewer resources. Focusing on EAM, or increase equipment efficiency,
maximizes capacity and financials. Understanding this is important if
companies are going to be competitive in the next decade.

Some companies are beginning to clearly understand this, as shown
by some of the latest maintenance key performance indicators that they
utilize. For example, they measure maintenance cost (MC) as a percentage of the estimated replacement value of the assets (ERV). This calculation is shown in Figure 8-3. The maintenance cost compared to the estimated replacement value is calculated by dividing the total maintenance
costs by the total asset valuation. This percentage is then used to evaluate
if the proper level of expenditures is being made for maintenance and reliability.

Why is spending to improve maintenance and reliability important
to a CMMS / EAM implementation? Research performed by Professor
Brynjolfsson at MIT Sloan School of Management provides the answer.
Professor Brynjolfsson's research showed that when companies make

Maintenance Costs as a Percentage of
Estimated Replacement Value

$$MC/ERV = \frac{\text{Maintenance Costs}}{\text{Total Asset Valuation}}$$

Figure 8-3

investments in ERP systems, about five times as much is spent on improving business processes, and training and education of workers, as is spent on the software and hardware. The reason is that no business improvement can be made simply by implementing a computer system. Implementing the system, coupled with improving business processes, will produce the desired return on investment and ultimately the increase in profitability. Professor Brynjolfsson's research further made this point when he showed that the true capacity of companies that make business process improvements are as if they have invisible factories or hidden capacity. His study showed that there is an estimated $2 trillion in additional productive capacity in the United States, which does not show up in GDP statistics or on the balance sheet of companies.

Unfortunately, maintenance and reliability is a function within the majority of corporations that most people do not understand. Complicating the matter even more is that too many people think they understand the maintenance function. This misunderstanding is evident by the many differing methods currently used to organize and perform maintenance in all corporations. Most corporate and plant executives have concentrated on operations or manufacturing management, whereas management of the more technical disciplines such as maintenance have been ignored or placed in a secondary status. Maintenance, for example, has been viewed as a necessary evil or insurance policy, where money is paid and nothing (in their lifetime) is ever seen as a return.

In an effort to become more competitive, managers are turning over every stone to find areas for improvement and cost savings. As they study the maintenance function, companies have found that maintenance makes up anywhere from 15% to 40% of total product cost. They are also discovering that dollars saved in maintenance are a cost avoidance. If they take the typical profit margins for manufacturing companies, they discover one dollar saved in maintenance costs contributes as much to company profits as $3.00 in new sales. In larger companies, reducing maintenance expenditures by $1 million contributes as much to profits as increasing sales by $3 million. In the competitive markets all companies find themselves, being able to improve maintenance and decrease unnecessary maintenance expenditures by $1 million is much easier and likely to occur than finding $3 million in new sales.

The following material presents guidelines for calculating possible financial benefits a company may achieve by implementing improved maintenance policies and practices, including utilizing a CMMS / EAM system. Author's Note: It must be clear that implementing a CMMS / EAM system without improving maintenance and reliability practices will not produce any significant financial benefits.

This chapter presents a structured examination of the effect of maintenance on a company's finances. The material is divided to allow for various components to be used where applicable and omitted where not. This structure will allow companies to customize the return on investment justification to meet their own circumstances.

Standard Cost Justification

This portion of the cost justification is composed of the following four main parts:
- Maintenance labor costs
- Maintenance materials costs
- Project cost savings
- Downtime / Availability costs

Maintenance Labor Costs

Maintenance productivity in most American companies averages 20–30%. This amount translates into approximately 2 hours per 8 hour shift of hands-on activities. Most of the lost productivity can be attributed

to the following reasons:
- Waiting on parts

- Waiting on information, drawings, instructions, etc.

- Waiting for the equipment to be shut down

- Waiting on rental equipment to arrive

- Waiting on other crafts to finish their part of the job

- Running from emergency to emergency

Although 100% productivity is an unrealistic goal for any maintenance organization, a more realistic percentage of 60% is achievable.

The productivity of maintenance technicians can be improved by concentrating on basic management techniques, such as:
- Planning jobs in advance

- Scheduling jobs and coordinating schedules with operations

- Arranging for the parts to be ready

- Coordinating the tools, rental equipment, etc.

- Reducing the emergency work below the 50% level by PM

With computer assistance, planning time per job is reduced, resulting in more jobs planned and coordinated. This results in more time for preventive maintenance activities, which in turn helps to reduce the amount of emergency and breakdown activities. This results in fewer schedule changes and helps to increase the productivity by reducing travel and waiting times. Successful organizations using CMMS / EAM systems have indicated an increase in productivity of 28%.

Maintenance Material Costs

The material costs are related to the frequency and size of the repairs made to the company's equipment. The sheer number of parts, in addition to the stores policies, purchasing policies, and overall inventory management practices, contribute to the overall maintenance materials costs. Because little attention is paid to maintenance materials in some companies, inventories may be higher than necessary by some 20–30%. This amount increases inventory holding costs and makes materials unnecessarily expensive. The inability of the stores to service the maintenance department's needs results in "pirate" or 'illegal" storage depots for just-in-case spares. This practice also drives up the cost of maintenance materials. Typical material-related wastes are listed in Figure 8-4. With materials making up 50% of the total maintenance costs, this area is one where improvement is necessary.

Material-Related Wastes

- Waiting on materials
- Travel time to obtain materials
- Time to transport materials to job site
- Time to identify untagged materials
- Time to find substitute materials
- Time to find parts in remote/ alternative locations
- Time to obtain purchase order approvals
- Cost of processing purchase order
- Time lost due to:
    - Other crafts having material problems
    - Wrong materials planned, ordered, or delivered
    - Materials out of stock

Figure 8-4

Good inventory controls enables companies to lower the value of the inventory and still maintain a service level of at least 95%. The maintenance department can then be responsive to the operations group, while increasing their own personal productivity. Successful CMMS / EAM system users have averaged 19% lower material costs and an overall 18% reduction in total inventory.

Project Cost Savings

In many companies, maintenance is involved in project, outage, or refurbishing activities. These activities, if not properly controlled, can have a dramatic impact on a company's production capacity. The reason for this is that these activities are usually performed with the equipment in a down condition, when there is no production. Therefore, any time that can be eliminated from the project, outage, or refurbishing can be converted back into to production time. In the refining and power generation business, the cost of a prolonged outage is prohibitive.

Improved planning and coordination can be achieved with a CMMS / EAM system. These efforts will often help to shorten the downtime, even if the company is currently using a project management system. Successful CMMS/ EAM system users have indicated an average 5% reduction in outage time.

Downtime/Availability Costs

These costs are the true savings for a company determined to improve maintenance policies and practices. Downtime cost for equipment may vary from several thousands of dollars per hour to literally hundreds of thousands of dollars per hour. One company has several production lines in their plant, with the downtime on each being worth $1 M for 24 hours.

In some companies, levels of downtime can run as high as 30% or more. Downtime results in lost sales opportunities and unnecessary expenditures for capital equipment. It generally puts the company in a weak competitive position. By dedicating the company to enforcing good maintenance policies and practices and utilizing the CMMS / EAM system as a tracking tool, equipment downtime can be reduced dramatically. Successful CMMS / EAM system users have averaged a 20% reduction in equipment downtime losses.

The following section presents forms that can be used to calculate the return on investment for a maintenance improvement project, including implementing a CMMS / EAM system. For each question, guidelines are presented with maintenance department averages, based on various industry studies and actual plant case studies.

Survey #1: Maintenance Labor Costs

1. Time wasted by personnel looking for spare equipment parts

(Averages)   _____
       No inventory system   = 15–25%
       Manual Inventory System =10–20%
       Work order system and
         inventory system   =5–15%
       Computerized inventory and
         manual work order system = 0–5%

2. Time spent looking for information about a work order

                                           _____
       Manual WO system   =5–15%
       No WO system   = 10–20%

3. Time wasted by starting wrong priority work order _____
       Manual WO system   = 0–5%
       No WO System   = 5–10%

4. Time wasted by equipment not being ready to work on
  (still in production)   _____
       Manual WO system   = 0–5%
       No WO system   = 10–15%

5. Total of all percentages of wasted time   _____
     (#1 + #2 + #3 + #4)

6. Total number of craftsmen   _____

7. Multiply this figure (# 6) times 2080 (normal hours
  worked by an employee for a year)   _____

8. Multiply the percentage totals times the total number
  of hours for all craftsmen (#5 x #7)   _____

9. Enter the average labor rate including benefits
   for a craftsman (sometimes called burden rate)   _____

10. Multiply the potential savings in hours times the
    average labor rate (#9 x #8)   _____

11. Multiply the figure in line 10 time the percentage
    from the table below that best describes your facility
       No WO or inventory system   = 75–100%
       Manual WO system   =50–75%
       Manual WO and inventory system = 30–50%
       Computerized inventory and
       manual WO system   =25–40%   _____

12.   TOTAL SAVINGS   _____

This figure represents the projected savings for increasing labor productivity by improving maintenance practices and implementing a CMMS / EAM system.

Explanation of Survey #1 (Maintenance Labor Costs)
The explanation for the labor cost justification follows the form's steps.
Step 1, you enter the total percentage of time the craftsmen are engaged in looking for materials. Each company will have varying averages depending on their current material control system and the level of reactive maintenance and advanced planning functions. It is not necessary to time study the maintenance technicians; a good estimate will suffice. The time wasted should include lost time at the start of a job, during the job, and after a job when returning unused materials to the stores.
Step 2 is the time spent trying to determine exactly what work was requested on the work order. This is caused by insufficient work order descriptions such as "It's broke, fix it" or "Repair or replace as necessary." The more vague that the work order is, or the fewer details on the work

order, the higher the percentage of time technicians will spend looking for additional details.

Step 3 is the time spent due to fluctuating priorities. If the technicians start one job in the morning and, after starting it, are pulled off to work on other jobs that someone now believes are more important than the original job, there is a subsequent loss of productivity. The more often technicians are moved from job to job, the higher this percentage of wasted time will be.

Step 4 is the percentage of time wasted when technicians go out to the job and the operations or production department then change their schedule and will not release the equipment for maintenance. This type of delay occurs more frequently in plants where breakdowns cause production departments to frequently alter their schedules.

Step 5 is the total of all the waste percentages. If you have other types of productivity wastes, you should add this percentage of wasted productivity to the number in this step. Again, this figure may be as high as 50–80%.

Step 6 is the total number of craft technicians at the site who will be affected by the CMMS / EAM system or using it for planning and scheduling.

Step 7 is the product from multiplying the number of technicians in Step 6 by the average hours worked in a year by the technicians. This figure is 2080 hours for a straight 40-hour week for an entire year.

Step 8 is the result of multiplying the total number of hours worked by all technicians from Step 7 by the total of all the wasted time percentages from Step 5. This product gives the total number of labor hours wasted in a year

Step 9 is the average labor rate for the technicians.

Step 10 is the product from multiplying the average labor rate from Step 9 and the total number of labor hours wasted in a year from Step 8. This product should show the potential savings in dollars for the labor.

Step 11 requires you to identify the present condition of your organization. Finding the correct range and then estimating your present level of control in the maintenance and stores area allow you to identify what part of the amount from Step 10 you will be likely to save.

Step 12 is the product from multiplying the percentage from Step 11 times the potential savings in dollars from Step 10. This product is the total dollar savings the CMMS / EAM system, coupled with the maintenance and reliability Best Practices, could make in your labor productivity.

Survey #2: Inventory and Stores Savings

1. Total dollar value of maintenance spares purchased per year

    _____

2. Percentage of time spares are already in stores
   when others are purchased

No inventory system	= 25–30%
Manual inventory system	= 10–20%
Computerized inventory system	= 5–15%

    _____

3. Savings total (cost avoidance)(#1 x #2)

    _____

4. Additional savings (inventory overhead)
   Multiply #3 times 30%

    _____

5. Estimated total inventory valuation

    _____

6. Estimated inventory reduction

No inventory system	= 15–20%
Manual system	= 5–10%

   (obsolete or unnecessary spares)

    _____

7. Estimated one-time inventory reduction
   Multiply # 5 x #6

    _____

8. Estimated additional savings
   Multiply #7 by 30% (holding cost reduction)

    _____

9. Number of stockouts causing downtime

    _____

10. Amount of downtime (in hours)

    _____

11. Cost of downtime (per hour)

    _____

12. Total cost of materials-related downtime
    Multiply #10 x #11

    _____

13. Percentage of savings obtainable

    _____

                Current controls poor   = 75%
                Current controls fair   = 50%
                Current controls good   = 25%

14. Savings in materials-related equipment downtime   _____
        Multiply #12 x # 13

15. TOTAL SAVINGS   _____
        Add # 3, #4, #7, #8, and #14

Explanation of Survey #2 (Inventory and Stores Savings)

The explanation of the stores savings begins with the total value of spare parts purchased each year. This number should be as accurate as possible and include all parts bought through plant purchasing, parts charged to blanket or open purchase orders, parts stocked or maintained by vendors, and parts ordered as direct buys.

Step 2 is the percentage of times the spare part could be found somewhere in the plant and, because it was not easily found or it was not known at the time where it was located, it was purchased unnecessarily. The percentages indicated are ranges to be used depending on the current status of the organization.

Step 3 is the value of the spare parts from Step 1 times the percentage indicated in Step 2. This is a cost-avoidance quantity; it applies mainly during the first year of CMMS / EAM system usage. After the first year, the stock quantities should be under more disciplined control.

Step 4 is the stock reduction from Step 3 times the average holding cost for spare parts. In most companies, 30% is an acceptable estimated holding cost percentage. If your actual holding cost percentage is known, use it instead of the 30% estimate.

Step 5 is the total dollar valuation of the inventory currently on hand for the company. This should include the "private" or "pirate" stores held by various employees or crews. It should also include all major spares as well as normal items. Any items put in long-term storage (graveyards or bone yards) should also be included.

Step 6 is the estimated reduction in total spares for the company. The percentages are based on the current mode of inventory control. The fewer the controls or the lower the adherence to the inventory control disciplines, the higher the percentage of waste that potentially could be eliminated.

Step 7 is the result of multiplying Step 5 by Step 6. This will be the estimated dollar reduction for the inventory. This amount will be a one-time inventory write down. This savings is typically the largest one a company will experience during the first year of the CMMS implementation.

Step 8 is derived by multiplying Step 7 by the same holding cost percentage used in Step 4. Again, in most plants, 30% is an acceptable value. If your actual holding cost percentage is known, you should use it.

Step 9 is the actual number of stockouts experienced by the stockroom that resulted in equipment downtime. This number should be less than the total number of stockouts. The less inventory control currently in use, the higher this number will be. In stockrooms with little or no control, the percentage of stockouts could be as high as 40% of all requests. The reverse of this figure is the service level. Correspondingly, the service level should be in the 60% range.

The percentage of these stockouts resulting in downtime is also proportional to the amount of reactive maintenance performed by the company. If the company has little inventory control and is operating with reactive maintenance, then as much as 50% of all stockouts could result in equipment downtime. This translates into 20% of all stockroom transactions resulting in an equipment delay. The range from reactive organizations to proactive organizations goes from 20% to 1% of total transactions resulting in equipment downtime. If you have actual, reliable percentages, they should be used.

Step 10 is the total equipment downtime resulting from the stockouts. If this number is known, it should be used. If this number is not known, it may derived by looking at all maintenance work orders resulting in equipment downtime and getting the percentage of all these work orders requiring materials. Using this number, in conjunction with the information from Step 9, a close approximation of the total stockout-related equipment downtime could be obtained. If these figures are not available, industry averages run from a high of 40% to a low (for organizations with good inventory controls) of 2%.

Step 11 is the average cost of downtime for the company's equipment. If an average amount is not available, it may be feasible (if good records are available) to calculate the actual downtime for each piece of equipment and enter the total for all equipment in Step 11.

Step 12 is the result of multiplying Step 10 and Step 11. This should result in the total material related downtime for the plant.

Step 13 is the percentage of the downtime likely to be eliminated by improved inventory controls. This percentage will be based on the current level of inventory controls. The percentages shown are industry averages.

Step 14 is the result of multiplying Step 12 by Step 13. This product should be the total equipment downtime costs that could be saved by implementing good inventory controls.

Step 15 is the sum of Steps 3, 4, 7, 8, and 13. This figure should be the total of all projected material savings for the company.

Survey #3: Major Project, Outage, and Overhaul Savings

1. Number of major outages and overhauls per year   _____

2. Average length (in days) of outage or overhaul   _____

3. Cost of equipment downtime in lost sales   _____
    (Use hourly downtime rate times total hours of outages)

4. Total estimated cost per year   _____
    Multiply #1, #2, and #3

5. Estimated savings percentage   _____
      No computerized WO system   =   5–10%
      Project management system   =   3–8%
      Project management system and
      Inventory control system   =   2–5%

6. TOTAL COST SAVINGS   _____
    Multiply #4 and #5

Explanation of Survey #3 (Major Project, Outage and Overhaul Savings)

Step 1 is the total number of major projects, outages, and overhauls that are completed each year. In order for the project, outage, or overhaul to be included in this total, it must result in equipment downtime, production loss, or delays.

Step 2 is the total number of days for all of the major projects, outages, and overhauls for the company. Again, these must be days of downtime for the equipment, resulting in production loss or delays.

Step 3 is the average cost of equipment downtime per day for the equipment impacted by the major projects, outages, and overhauls identified in Steps 1 and 2. These costs are usually incurred when the equipment capacity is required or the resulting downtime requires the product to be diverted or delayed.

Step 4 is the result of multiplying Step 2 and Step 3. This is the total equipment downtime costs for all of the major projects, outages, and overhauls for the company.

Step 5 is the percentage of the total equipment downtime related to major projects, outages, and overhauls for the company that could be saved if good maintenance controls were implemented. The averages are based on the controls currently utilized by the company.

Step 6 is the result of multiplying Step 4 and Step 5. This product represents the total projected saving from better controls on the company's major projects, outages, and overhauls.

Survey #4: Equipment Downtime Costs

1. Percentage of equipment downtime for year _____
   (If not known, use estimate; average for industry is 5–25%)

2. Total number of production hours for equipment for year

   _____

3. Total of all lost production hours for year
   (Multiply #1 and #2) _____

4. Multiply total lost production hours for year (from # 3) times your percentage from the table below. _____

Presently using:
No work order system   = 25%
Work order system   = 20%
Work order and stores inventory system = 10%

5. Total of downtime hours saved   _____

6. Cost of downtime for 1 hour   _____

7. TOTAL DOWNTIME COST SAVINGS   _____
       (Multiply #5 x #6)

   Optional Savings Considerations

8. Total direct labor wages and benefits times
    the total of all lost production hours   _____

9. Lost sales for year   _____
    (Divide the total sales for year by the total number of
    yearly production hours. Multiply this figure
    times the total downtime hours saved.)

10. Increased production costs to make up production lost _____
       due to downtime. (This include the extra labor required
       on week-ends or off shifts to operate the equipment,
       extra energy costs to operate the equipment, etc.)

Explanation of Survey #4 (Equipment Downtime Costs)
     Step 1 is the percentage of equipment downtime for the company. In order to obtain the total value for the plant equipment downtime, it may be necessary to calculate this section for the major critical pieces of equipment. The values given are industry averages. These should be used only if your actual downtime is not known.
     Step 2 is the total number of production hours the equipment was scheduled for the year. Because downtime is only accumulated when the equipment is scheduled to operate, this number must be derived from the production schedule.

Step 3 is the total number of lost production hours per year, obtained by multiplying Step 1 and Step 2.

Step 4 is the percentage of Step 3 that could possibly be saved by implementing good maintenance processes and the disciplined controls in a CMMS / EAM system. This percentage is based on the current condition of the company. The industry averages listed provide guidelines for the possible savings.

Step 5 is the result of multiplying the percentage in Step 4 and the lost production hours in Step 3. This product is the total number of downtime hours that are projected to be saved by implementing good maintenance processes and the disciplined controls in a CMMS / EAM system.

Step 6 is the cost of 1 hour of downtime for the production equipment used to compile the total in Step 3. This figure may vary from equipment to equipment within the plant. You may take an average cost for all of the equipment, or perform the calculations in this section for each individual piece of equipment, then total the individual sums.

Step 7 is the result of multiplying Step 5 by Step 6. This total is the downtime savings projected by implementing good maintenance processes and the disciplined controls in a CMMS / EAM system.

Step 8 is an optional consideration for downtime cost savings. It is the wages and benefits for the total number of idle operators hours incurred during the equipment downtime. This is typically calculated by multiplying the downtime hours times the number of operators assigned to the equipment. In some cases, this value is already added into the equipment downtime cost figure. If this is this case, this value should not be used.

Step 9 is another optional consideration for downtime cost savings. It is the value of the lost sales for the plant. This value is only usable if the plant is operating at full capacity and any downtime is a lost sales opportunity for the product. The value is the amount of the product not produced during the downtime.

Step 10 is another optional consideration for the downtime cost savings. It is the increased production costs to make up the product lost during the downtime. These costs are somewhat more difficult to determine, but would include the extra wages paid the operating and maintenance staffs to cover the new production times scheduled. This amount is usually 1.5 times their base rate. These costs also include the additional equipment utilities charges for operating the equipment when it should have been down. There are also other paperwork charges incurred for changing material flows, transferring materials from the equipment to storage and back to the equipment, etc.

If they are applicable, the value of Steps 8 through 10 should be added to the total in Step 7.

Survey #5: Total Projected Savings

1. Total from Survey #1   _____

2. Total from Survey #2   _____

3. Total from Survey #3   _____

4. Total from Survey #4   _____

5. TOTAL SAVINGS possible from system installation
   (Sum of lines #1–#4)   _____

6. Total projected price for system   _____
   (include hardware, software, support agreements,
   training, and implementation costs)

7. Payback (Divide #6 by #5)   _____

Detailed Cost Savings

The savings suggested in this section are somewhat more difficult to calculate for most companies because they require some data to be known or accurately estimated. When available, industry averages or ranges are given as guidelines for companies not possessing complete internal data.

Warranty Costs for Equipment

In many companies that have recently purchased equipment, warranty costs is an area of possible savings. In many instances, some of the maintenance repairs made on equipment under warranty are reimbursable under the purchase and service agreement with the equipment supplier. The amount of the reimbursement can vary, but companies have found that 5–10% of all work performed on equipment covered by warranties can be reimbursed.

A company will want to make certain considerations when investigating this area of savings. These areas may make the compliance with warranty provisions challenging. They are:

- To be covered by the warranty, do the repairs have to be made by or supervised by a representative of the supplier company?

- If the repairs are made by internal technicians, does it void the warranty?

- What level of documentation must be provided to the supplier to collect under the terms of the warranty?

If these or similar provisions would impact the warranty, the company may want to consider whether they are worth the effort. For example, what if a critical piece of equipment would have to remain shut down waiting for the supplier representative to arrive and make or oversee the repairs? The cost of the downtime would no doubt quickly exceed the moneys that could be regained from warranty claims.

There are opportunities to receive reimbursements for repairs made to equipment under warranty. However, a company will want to make a serious cost/benefit evaluation before these are actively pursued.

Energy Cost Savings

In order to effectively calculate any energy costs savings, companies must know their energy usage. If this is not known, industry averages can be used for a quick estimate of the savings. Studies by the engineering institutes and international companies have shown that companies can cut energy consumption at a plant by 5–10%, depending on their current maintenance effort. Companies with good maintenance programs would see savings in the 5% range. Companies with little or no preventive maintenance inspections and services would realize savings in the 10% range. Some examples of energy savings for typical systems follow.

Mechanical Systems

Some of the energy savings in mechanical systems are defined by the type of preventive maintenance performed on some of the basic mechanical components. For example, how accurate are couplings aligned? Misalignment by even 0.003" can lead to energy loss through the coupling. This loss is typically displayed as heat energy in the flex member of the coupling and the supporting shaft bearings. Even elastomer couplings will display energy loss.

A second type of mechanical loss comes from V-Belt slippage. Insufficient tension results in slippage during loading on the belt. This loss is again shown as heat in the contact area between the belt and the sheave. Chain and gear misalignment will also lose energy in the transmission area and bearings. Poor maintenance practices and preventive maintenance will contribute a 5–10% energy loss for mechanical power transmission.

Electrical Systems

As with mechanical systems, the energy waste in electrical systems will be determined by the condition of the electrical systems and the level of maintenance service performed on the systems. Typical energy losses occur in loose connections and poor motor conditions, including contamination insulating the motor, thereby increasing the temperature of the motor and subsequently its energy consumption.

Improper or insufficient maintenance on mechanical drives will also increase the amount of energy required by the motor to drive the system. This inefficiency, along with many other losses, will contribute to excessive energy requirements by electrical systems. As with mechanical systems, expect a 5–10% energy loss due to poor electrical system maintenance.

Steam Systems

Steam generations systems have long been recognized as having potential to produce substantial energy savings for most plants. Steam trap inspection programs, energy efficient boilers, and leak detection programs have been utilized in reducing steam system losses.

Depending on the amount of maintenance performed on the steam system, energy savings from 5–15% have been reported by companies initiating good maintenance practices.

Fluid Power Systems

Fluid power systems include both hydraulic and pneumatic systems. Energy wastes in these systems are generally related to leaks, which can be internal or external. External leaks are easier to find because air will make noise and oil leaves a pool of fluid. These leaks waste energy because the compressor or pump will have to run more frequently for the system to operate correctly. In addition, hydraulic systems will require cleaning up the leaks, another form of energy waste.

Internal leaks are more difficult to detect, particularly when the leaks are small. They are usually identified by sluggish performance and, in hydraulic systems, excessive component heat. Again, the pumps and compressors must run more frequently to compensate for the leaks. These inefficiencies and other energy losses will account for energy losses of 5–15% in fluid power systems.

As seen from these examples, a 5–10% energy reduction in the plant can easily be attained by a good preventive maintenance system.

Quality Cost Savings

Because the maintenance department is responsible for the equipment condition, quality costs are impacted by poor maintenance practices. For example, what percent of all quality problems are eventually solved by a maintenance activity? Even if the activity is performed by the operator, the activity is one of maintaining the equipment condition. In some companies, 60% or more of the quality problems are equipment related. In order to calculate the possible cost savings, the value of the annual production for the plant should be calculated. Next, the current first-pass quality rate should be determined. The difference between this rate and 100% gives the current reject rate.

The next step would be to determine the reasons for the rejects. Usually a top ten list will provide the majority of the rejects. After examining the list, determine which causes have a maintenance solution. This is the percentage amount that could possibly be reduced. An estimate of what percent of all the maintenance-related losses could be eliminated by a good maintenance program must be made. This percentage times the dollar value of the company's annual product will produce the possible quality-related savings. This number should then be added as a line item to all of the previous savings.

Paperwork / Clerical Savings

This section looks at the decrease in paperwork and clerical support that a CMMS requires compared to the current manual method that most organizations are using. The current time required may be supplied by maintenance clerks, planners, supervisors, or even the maintenance manager. If the responsibilities are spread over multiple individuals, use the average labor cost for the calculation. Surveys 6, 7, 8, and 9 cover different aspects of paperwork and clerical savings.

Survey #6: Maintenance Paperwork / Clerical Cost Justification

Use Weekly Averages

1. Amount of time to plan work orders _____

2. Amount of time to post time to work orders _____

3. Amount of time preparing management reports _____

4. Amount of time to update equipment histories _____

5. Amount of time to generate weekly schedules _____

6. Amount of time spent preparing PMs _____

7. Amount of time spent preparing
   bill of materials for the weekly schedule _____

8. Time spent on other maintenance-related
   clerical activities _____

9. Total maintenance-related paperwork /clerical
   time per week (total #1–8) _____

10. Anticipated reduction in clerical / paperwork
    time required (usually 20%) _____

11. Total hourly savings (multiply # 9 x #10) _____

12. Average hourly clerical / paperwork cost   _____

13. Total dollar savings from clerical / paperwork
    improvements (Multiply #11 x #12)   _____

Survey #7: Clerical / Paperwork Savings for Stores / Inventory

Use Weekly Averages

1. Amount of time to issue parts to work orders   _____

2. Amount of time to post material charges
   to work orders   _____

3. Amount of time preparing inventory reports   _____

4. Amount of time to perform receiving functions   _____

5. Amount of time to restock inventory items   _____

6. Amount of time spent staging WO materials   _____

7. Amount of time spent performing window
   issues for maintenance materials   _____

8. Time spent on other inventory-related
   clerical activities   _____

9. Total inventory-related paperwork / clerical
   time per week (total #1–8)   _____

10. Anticipated reduction in clerical / paperwork
    time required (usually 20%)   _____

11. Total hourly savings (multiply #9 x #10)   _____

12. Average hourly clerical / paperwork cost   _____

13. Total dollar savings from clerical / paperwork   _____
improvements (Multiply #11 x #12)   _____

Survey #8: Clerical / Paperwork Savings for Purchasing

Use Weekly Averages

1. Amount of time to prepare purchase requisitions   _____

2. Amount of time to consolidate purchase requisitions   _____

3. Amount of time preparing purchase orders   _____

4. Amount of time to update purchase order history   _____

5. Amount of time to generate purchasing reports   _____

6. Amount of time spent contacting vendors for pricing   _____

7. Time spent on other purchasing-related   _____
clerical activities

8. Total purchasing-related paperwork / clerical   _____
time per week (total #1–7)

9. Anticipated reduction in clerical / paperwork   _____
time required (usually 20%)

10. Total hourly savings (multiply # 8 x #9)   _____

11. Average hourly clerical / paperwork cost   _____

12. Total dollar savings from clerical / paperwork   _____
improvements (multiply #10 x #11)

Survey #9: Clerical / Paperwork Savings for Engineering

Use Weekly Averages

1. Amount of time to find drawings for work orders   _____

2. Amount of time to update equipment drawings   _____

3. Amount of time updating PM program   _____

4. Amount of time performing failure analysis   _____

5. Amount of time performing reliability engineering   _____

6. Amount of time spent providing information
   to the maintenance organization   _____

7. Time spent on other maintenance-related
   engineering clerical activities   _____

8. Total maintenance engineering-related
   paperwork / clerical time per week (total #1–7)   _____

9. Anticipated reduction in clerical / paperwork
   time required (usually 20%)   _____

10. Total hourly savings (multiply #8 x #9)   _____

11. Average hourly clerical / paperwork cost   _____

12. Total dollar savings from clerical / paperwork
    improvements (multiply # 10 x #11)   _____

New Capital Investment Savings

This section of the cost justification will require the budget for capital equipment replacement for the current year or the projection for the next year. Once this information is known, it is necessary to know the current type of maintenance activities. For example, is the company reactive or proactive in its maintenance practices? Is the company currently utilizing good preventive and predictive techniques? The formula for calculating this savings is as follows:

NCR\$ x A% = Projected Savings in New Capital Investment

NCR\$ = New Capital Replacement Dollars Budgeted

A% =   The percent savings to be achieved.
This percent is based on the current condition
of the maintenance organization.
Currently reactive = 30%
Preventive = 20%
Preventive and Predictive = 10%

Additional Purchasing Savings

There are three main areas under consideration in this section. Whether these savings can be used by any company depends if the described function currently exists. The three areas are:

- Buyer performance

- Volume pricing from vendors

- Blanket supplier contracts

Buyer performance can be increased by as much as 25% if a company doesn't have a good maintenance planning and scheduling system in place. Calculating the savings for this area uses the formula:

$$\frac{\# \text{ of Buyers } x \ \# \text{ of hours spent (each) on maintenance purchasing}}{x \ \text{Savings\%} \ = \ \text{Total Hours Saved}}$$

Multiplying the total hours saved by the hourly rate for the buyers will provide the total dollar savings for the increased buyer performance.

The volume pricing from the vendors is obtained by tracking the total volume of business awarded each vendor for the year and negotiating discount percentages on future purchases. This technique is only successful if the number of vendors is narrowed to a select few and close track of all expenditures is kept. Depending on the level of business with the vendor, discounts of 3–10% are possible. This percentage would be calculated for the volume of business done with each vendor.

The effective use of blanket contracts will allow the vendor to store many of the plants spares and supplies in their warehouse and only charge the company upon usage. There are no holding costs and the size of the inventory can be reduced. Many companies have successfully made this type of arrangement with fasteners, bearings, and other power transmission components. The supplier also guarantees delivery within so many hours of the order. In return, the company must guarantee the supplier a certain level of business each year.

Additional Inventory Savings

The additional inventory savings described in this section will be divided into three areas. The amount of savings in each area depends on the current status of the organization and how much is currently spent in these areas. These areas are:

- Greater inventory turnover

- Reduced order expediting

- Better pricing from vendors

Currently the average for maintenance inventory turns in the United States is about .75 per year. World Class is considered to be 1 turn per year. Turning the inventory over more frequently allows more capital to be free for investment. Calculating the savings in this area requires knowing both the total inventory valuation and the number of turns per year currently. The difference between the calculated number and the goal of 1 turn per year should be multiplied by the dollar value of the current inventory on hand and this will be the possible savings in this area. For example, if the goal is 1 turn and the current level is .75, then .25 times the total inventory valuation (use $10M for example) the possible saving would be $2.5M

Savings can also come from reducing the number of orders that are expedited. Achieving these savings will require knowing the amount of money spent on expediting spares parts for maintenance in the last year. The savings will depend on the current amount of reactive or short term maintenance being performed. However, an average organization can expect a 50% reduction in expediting costs the first year.

The ability of the CMMS to track regular, blanket, and emergency purchases will help to identify the total dollar volume of business done with any single vendor. Having this information will allow for negotiations with the vendor for a volume discount based on the total business done with the vendor. As mentioned in the purchasing section, discounts of 3% to 10% are customary.

Additional Accounts Payable Savings

The additional savings in the accounts payable area can be divided into the following three areas:

- Reduced invoice errors

- More accurate and timely payments to vendors

- Increased accounting accuracy

Reduced invoice errors come from having accurate information about how invoices travel from ordering to purchasing to receiving to accounts payable. The computerized flow should reduce the invoice error level to below 2% of all invoices. Industry estimates show it takes 1 hour of clerical time to correct an invoicing error. By comparing a company's present error level and estimating the savings if it is reduced, a possible dollar value can be derived.

The savings for more accurate and timely payments to the vendors also results from having accurate information electronically available to all groups involved in the transaction. Reducing the errors and late payments can help the company avoid any overdue or unpaid charges from the vendors. The savings could be estimated by examining those charges for the last year and projecting a reduction of errors to the 1–3% level of all transactions. Examining the late charges in this light should show the resulting savings.

Savings from Increased accounting accuracy are based on the electronic accuracy of the information in the system. Additional billing and receiving errors should be eliminated, with the savings based on the current error level in the company. Here too, a 1–3% error level is easily achievable.

THE FUTURE OF CMMS/EAM SYSTEMS

What is the future direction for CMMS / EAM systems? What are their trends? Should a company invest now or in the future?

These are all questions that face every company. Briefly we will consider some observations in these regards.

First, the buy now or later question is always asked. It is a waste of money not to implement a CMMS / EAM system and begin the savings immediately, provided the organization is ready. CMMS / EAM systems can be upgraded or changed as new enhancements are made. The importance is selecting a capable and qualified vendor, one that is willing to support their product from the beginning. With this being the case, what are some of the trends for the future?

CMMS / EAM System Trends

An overview of where CMMS / EAM systems are headed provides some interesting insights into the status of maintenance management. Currently, CMMS / EAM systems vendors are focusing in the following areas:

1. Support for TPM

2. Support for Predictive Systems

3. Utilization of Expert Systems

4. Interfaces with CAD and Imaging Systems

5. Integration with Production Scheduling Systems (MRP / MRPII)

Support for TPM

One of the current trends in maintenance management is the shift towards Total Productive Maintenance. This concept ties together the various parts of an organization around the utilization of equipment. The benchmark to this concept is the overall equipment effectiveness formula. The formula requires the delay times for the equipment, the capacity utilization rate, and the quality rate. Currently, most vendors offering this option require the user to manually enter the data from different systems. The future will allow the CMMS / EAM system to interface directly with the production scheduling control system to provide the input electronically. This feature is enhanced by allowing access to the CMMS / EAM system data by all involved personnel. Such access requires the vendors to insure their software has easy-to-use features insuring that all personnel can utilize the system for data entry and analysis.

Support for Predictive Systems

Although some vendors have offered the ability to pass data from predictive systems to the CMMS / EAM systems, the interfaces are becoming more sophisticated. Some of the latest interfaces allow for automatic Preventive Maintenance service order generation based on the current reading from the predictive system, with some allowing for repair work order generation automatically, if the condition becomes too severe. In addition to predictive interfaces, several vendors have developed real-time interfaces for their systems to allow input from PLCs (Programmable Logic Controllers) to trigger a maintenance request, similar to what the predictive systems will generate.

Utilization of Expert Systems

Several vendors are currently offering the ability to set troubleshooting guides or tables within their software, allowing the user this rough form of an expert system as a start. Future enhancements to their systems include tying this system to the equipment histories, thereby allowing for probabilities of failures and performing statistical analysis. Other vendors are working with troubleshooting and expert system vendors to develop interfaces, allowing for the power of these tools to be accessible to the maintenance and engineering organizations.

Interfaces with CAD and Imaging Systems

Some vendors have offered interfaces with Computer-Aided Design systems, (such as Autocad) for several years; however, the level of sophistication and ease of use of these features are increasing. The newer interfaces link the drawings to the equipment records, providing the users with quicker, easier access to the drawing information. The use of imaging system interfaces enables users to store not only drawings, but also part information and details, vendor's equipment manuals, and other technical information on the computer system. Users can then access the information from any appropriate terminal in the plant, eliminating the need to go to a technical library to retrieve information. The ability to access this information will help expedite repair and replacement.

Integration with ERP Systems

For the Best of Breed CMMS vendors, this is a sophisticated interface. Even for the Integrated suppliers, it is complex topic because a company must have excellent ERP scheduling practices in place as well as accurate schedule compliance for the maintenance organization (at least 95% compliance). Because only a minority of U.S. companies have had successful with ERP implementations and even fewer companies have "Best Practice" maintenance organizations, this integration is not fully utilized.

For example, in many integrated organizations, departments implement work-arounds such as blanket or department charge accounts for collecting costs they can not post to a work order. This practice corrupts the equipment cost histories and failure information. Although this full integration and great data integrity has been discussed by consultants, it is highly oversold because few companies achieve this level of proficiency with both the production and maintenance organizations. Only the future will determine the value of this type of integration to the manufacturing and process environments.

ISO-9000 Certification

The ISO-9000 is a set of suggested standards that businesses are being asked to comply with by the European marketplace. These standards are identified as:

ISO-9000 Organizations and Nomenclature
ISO-9001 Design/Development, Production, Installation, and
          Servicing
ISO-9002 Production and Installation
ISO-9003 Final Inspection and Test
ISO-9004 Quality System Guidelines

These standards, when complied with, provide assurance to all customers that the company's product meets high quality standards. How do the standards involve maintenance? It has been clearly shown you can't produce quality products on poorly-maintained equipment. When worn bearings or high wear areas exceed normal tolerances, then products will be hard to keep within specification. But, we don't need ISO-9000 to teach us this.

The side of ISO-9000 that some people will overlook is the record keeping and documentation to prove the production process is in control. For example, the 9004 standard covers the calibration and certification of all measuring and test equipment involved in producing the product. The standard highlights the need to identify the following: instruments, re-calibration schedule, recall procedures, calibration instructions, installation, and use. In addition, when instruments are found outside acceptable limits, the cause for the deviation is to be determined and a solution to prevent any reoccurrence is to be implemented.

More Distant Future

The more distant future seems to be moving toward the automated factory. Maintenance will be a key factor there. Already, system vendors are providing interfaces to the system for equipment monitoring. As the equipment needs it, it requests its own maintenance based on given engineering parameters set at installation.

The future trends in the systems seem to be integration of all modules in the systems. The technology already exists for almost all disparate systems in a plant to share data. It should eventually be possible to integrate CMMS / EAM systems with almost any computer system in the factory.

During the development of any maintenance tools, there are growth and development cycles. For example, take the development of vibration analysis equipment. At first, this equipment was very complex, difficult to use, and required extensive training to be proficient. As the products matured, the equipment became easier to use, the data became easier to understand, and the systems made predictive maintenance programs easier to manage.

Just as the predictive maintenance systems have improved and advanced, the CMMS / EAM systems have also showed the same trend. Recently, several major vendors in the marketplace have introduced new products or features to their present product lines that indicate the next generation of maintenance software is now arriving.

Functionality

The definition of the term functionality, as applied to maintenance management systems, is the activity controlled or monitored by the software. As any beginners shopping for their first maintenance software package can attest, most of the packages have standardized on the same functionality. They all seem to have the same basic components. These include:

1. Work Orders

2. Preventive Maintenance

3. Equipment Information

4. Inventory

5. Purchasing

6. Reports

If you were to talk to 20 or 30 vendors and request their literature, reading it would produce an overlapping matrix of information. The varying-sized systems would all sound alike, yet show a big difference in price. The prospective buyer would then ask, "What is the difference?" The difference is how the software accomplishes its task. When comparing systems, ask the following questions:

- How many keystrokes does it take to enter a work order?

- How many reference or "cheat" sheets does the user have to refer to in order to perform a function?

- How much manual manipulation of the data is required to achieve the desired results?

These types of questions will begin to show the differences. So, whereas most of the main functions are standardized within the systems, the steps the users have to take vary dramatically.

Some options being included in the "future" packages include:

1.   Maintenance Scheduling.
Some systems merely produce lists of work orders in the craft backlog; others have sophisticated scheduling algorithms allowing the com-

puter to do what it does best: analyze and sort data. The most recent generation of maintenance software packages are providing user-defined scheduling parameters to produce schedules set to the priorities established at each of the client sites. This allows for maximum flexibility and utilization of the maintenance workforce. They have the flexibility to schedule by craft, crew, department, or other parameters, making the schedule more useful in ERP, JIT, and CIM environments.

2.   *Analysis Reports.*

In the past, most reports were unintelligent lists. In the new systems, reports are meaningful, producing information such as exception reports, statistical analysis, and optimization reports.

3.   *Mobile Devices.*

Mobile devices are handheld devices which can be anything from a small computer to a Palm or Blackberry type device that can be used to download and upload information. The usage of these devices is already growing in the CMMS / EAM system marketplace. This is especially true in organizations where operators and maintenance personnel perform route inspections or need remote access to the work order system. The handheld device can synchronize with the CMMS / EAM System, or download the work orders or inspections that need to be performed. The operator or maintenance technician can then perform the inspections or work, and complete it electronically on the handheld device. Once the operator or technician is back in range of the main system, the handheld device synchronizes the data, uploading the information that was entered. These devices have been increasing in functionality at about the same rate as cell phone and I-Pod features. The future looks bright in this area.

4.   *Predictive Maintenance Enhancements.*

Vendors are enhancing existing predictive maintenance systems to provide transfer of information. This improvement allows some trigger in the predictive maintenance system to produce a work order in the computerized maintenance management system to correct a potential problem. Several vendors have working versions of this type of system in operation.

5.   *Interfaces vs. Integration.*

This is a lesson in semantics. Most vendors will say they can integrate their package with just about any other existing software package.

But, is that what they really mean? An interface is the passing of data between two systems. The data is generally then acted on in a batch mode. By contrast, integration is a real-time transfer of data between two systems. Each system will respond immediately to the data instead of waiting for a certain process to be run. It is easier and quicker to integrate the data with new generation software than with some of the older systems.

The prospective buyers must keep the following point in mind. Almost all CMMS / EAM systems interface; very few have working models of integration. In addition, integration is much more expensive than interfacing. You should be sure of your needs when asking for interfaces or integration.

System Features

User interfaces is a common buzz-word. It basically means the tools a user has to work within the system. User interfaces include pop-up windows, point and shoot selections, touch screens, and graphics. When examining these features, we find they have several advantages.

Pop-up Windows

Pop-up windows allow the vendor to program data windows to appear when the user is inputting data into key fields. The windows will usually contain the allowed entries for the field. This removes the necessity for the users to have an open manual at their terminals or to have a cheat sheet taped to their work stations. The pop-up windows may also be used to bring up help screens, other program information, or messages from other users.

Point and Shoot

Point and Shoot selections are often used on pop-up windows or on information inquiry screens. Point and shoot selections allow the user to move the highlighted bar up or down the screen; then, when the desired selection is highlighted, the user can press another key to insert the selection into the desired field. No retyping of the selection is required. This insures the data is accurate and reduces the amount of typing required by the user. The Point and Shoot selections and Pop-up Windows are trademarks of software written in 4th-generation languages.

Touch Screens

Touch screen technologies have existed for some time, but have just recently been applied to maintenance management software. Touch screens allow the user to answer a question, choose from a menu, or highlight a graphic display merely by touching a pre-defined section of the computer screen. Because this is more of a hardware function than a software function, most systems can use this technology. However, there is a difference between being able to use the technology and having written a software package to take advantage of the technology. Using it to operate a standard menu-driven system is different than using it with a system adapted for touch screen technology.

For example, one system allows the user to look at a graphical display of the plant, press a general geographical area, and have the area displayed in more detail. From the detailed diagram (usually an equipment layout) users can press the piece of equipment they desire. The system will then allow users to write a work order, look at equipment parts, or examine the equipment history. One system even lists a selection of typical problems for the piece of equipment. Then, after the user selects one, the system fills out a work order automatically. The ease-of-use rating for that system would have to be very high.

The down side of touch screen technologies for a maintenance or general plant environment is that you have to have clean hands. Otherwise, you spend the time you gain using touch screens cleaning the screen so you can see what you are doing. Only time will tell how useful and how much acceptance this technology receives.

Graphic Displays

Graphic displays of maintenance analysis information are also a mark of the next generation of CMMS / EAM systems. The days of looking at columns of figures have given way to days of enhanced graphs displaying trends or total information pictures. For example, it's much easier to look at a graph of the maintenance backlog for the last 6 months than it is the totals column. Graphs and charts make much more effective management presentations and reports than do pages of lists. Graphic displays of maintenance data are constantly gaining popularity and even now are an integral part of most CMMS / EAM systems. A sample graphical display screen is pictured in Figure 9-1.

Portals

The one feature that is bridging this section and the next is the use of portals. Portals are system front ends that allow the user to open an internet browser, such as Microsoft's Internet Explorer and access various computer system data. The browser displays different panes of data from various databases, allowing users to see on one screen all of the information they need to make decisions or to perform their job functions. The data can be drawn from various systems in the plant, including the ERP system, the CMMS / EAM system, the process control system, or any other system with the data necessary to allow the user to perform their job. A sample portal screen is shown in Figure 9-2.

The Far Distant Future

What will the maintenance management software of the future achieve that we don't have today? The following are often overheard discussed by Research and Development staffs:

- Artificial Intelligence and Expert Systems

- Enhancements for different organizational environments

- More sophisticated and enhanced hardware and software combinations

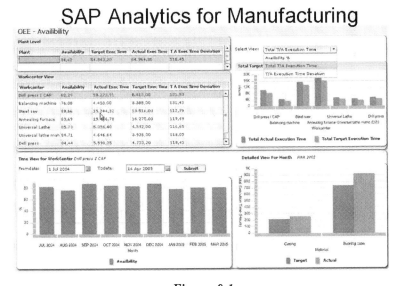

Figure 9-1

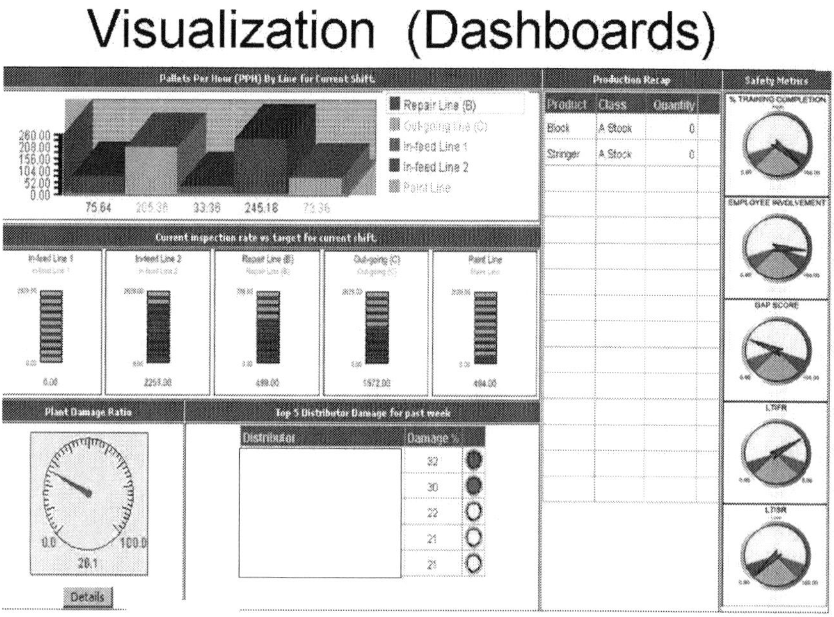

Visualization (Dashboards)

Figure 9-2

Artificial intelligence and expert systems have many different meanings, depending on the person you are speaking to. However, to CMMS / EAM systems users, they will be guides to equipment troubleshooting and repair. For example, if a problem developed on an equipment component, the repair person could go to a menu for the type of equipment. By selecting the symptoms the equipment is displaying, the solution to the problem could be derived. The main obstacle to utilizing this type of software is capturing all of the knowledge necessary to troubleshoot and repair equipment. This information resides in the current maintenance workforce, including technicians, supervisors, and maintenance engineers. This information must be captured and entered into a rules engine to drive the decision making process. It is interesting to watch this feature develop. Some vendors have been able to develop prototypes of these systems. A sample reliability screen is shown in Figure 9-3.

Enhancements for various environments will be developed, such as systems for companies with Total Productive Maintenance, ERP, Lean, Computer Integrated Manufacturing and Just-In-Time plants. These will be written to enable the users to optimize their performance in each environment. The information and user interfaces for these systems will be a

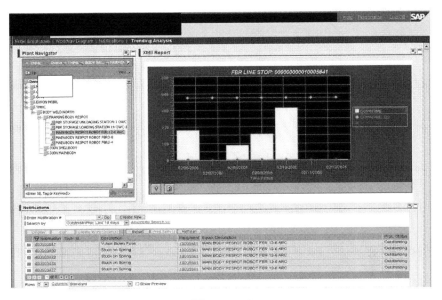

Figure 9-3

challenge to develop. Again, these areas will be interesting to watch develop.

Hardware and software operating systems and languages are another area where changes are frequently occurring. The development from the IBM-PC to the XT, the AT, and now the new multiple processor configurations occurred over a relatively short time period. However, look at the amount of power now available for an economical price. Tasks that used to take large mainframe computers considerable time to accomplish can now be quickly solved by small computers at a fraction of the cost. The future holds new processors, new computers, and new software languages. How the CMMS / EAM systems vendors will apply this technology is the third area that deserves attention in the future.

Conclusion

As past maintenance markets have grown and matured, it now seems the computerized maintenance management systems market is taking steps to achieve that goal. With the demands that the factories of the future, world market competition, TPM, Lean, ERP, and JIT environments are putting on maintenance organizations, the maturing is essential.

As the vendors work to increase the quality of the software to meet world class standards, the question becomes: Are we doing the same for our maintenance organizations and the people that comprise them?

10

PERFORMANCE INDICATORS FOR CMMS/EAM SYSTEMS

Computerized Maintenance Management Systems (CMMS) and Enterprise Asset Management Systems (EAM) are, in reality, nothing more than computerized versions of a maintenance information system. In fact, anything that can be done with a CMMS /EAM system can be done in a manual system. Using the computer, however, should make it faster and easier to collect data and then manipulate that data into a meaningful report format.

Recall from Figure 1-1 that the work order is the key feature of the system. It collects all of the labor data, the materials data, the contractor data, and the preventive maintenance data that is written against a piece of equipment (or a facility, building, floor, or room). The information collected is then stored in a database called the equipment history. It is from here that all of the data is drawn to produce all of the reports needed by the organization to manage its equipment or assets.

However, a study conducted by Engineer's Digest highlighted a problem. The majority of organizations owning and using a CMMS used only 50–60% of it. The question now is: What parts of the CMMS can you not use, without compromising the integrity of the data in the equipment history database? For example,

- If you don't record labor data, is the cost history accurate?

- If you don't record material data, is the cost history accurate?

- Could you perform life cycle costing?

- Could you calculate the MTBF?

- Could you calculate the MTTR?

The answer is, of course, no. Therefore, full use of the CMMS is necessary if any usable data is to be collected. The following indicators should be utilized to insure full and accurate data collection.

1. Percentage of Maintenance Labor Costs Recorded in CMMS/EAM System

This indicator compares the maintenance labor costs captured in the CMMS to the maintenance labor costs captured in the accounting system. If the CMMS is part of or integrated to an Enterprise Resource Planning system (ERP), then the reconciliation is not optional; the costs must match. This indicator insures that all labor costs are being recorded correctly.

$$\frac{\text{Total Maintenance Labor Costs in CMMS*}}{\text{Total Maintenance Labor Costs from Accounting}}$$

This indicator is derived by dividing the maintenance costs recorded in the CMMS by the maintenance labor costs in the accounting system. The resulting percentage is the degree of accuracy the labor data has in the CMMS. If the percentage is above 100%, then somehow the maintenance department is overbilling for its services. If the percentage is below 100%, then the maintenance department is not recording all of its labor activities.

Strengths

This indicator is mandatory for any company striving to insure complete accuracy of its maintenance labor charges.

Weaknesses

The weakness of this indicator is that sometimes it forces a maintenance organization to try to balance the numbers. At times, the organization may open a standing or blanket work order as a quick fix to try to cover the differences in the systems. This action should not be done. The real issue is that somewhere the labor data is not being recorded accurately against the appropriate equipment item. The errors should be traced and corrected.

2. Percentage of Maintenance Material Costs Recorded in CMMS / EAM System

This indicator is similar to the previous one except that it compares the maintenance material costs captured in the CMMS to the maintenance material costs captured in the accounting system. If the CMMS is part of or integrated to an ERP, or even a general ledger system, then the reconciliation is not optional; the costs must match. This indicator insures that all material costs are being recorded correctly.

$$\frac{\text{Total Maintenance Material Costs in CMMS*}}{\text{Total Maintenance Material Costs from Accounting}}$$

This indicator is derived by dividing the maintenance material costs recorded in the CMMS by the maintenance material costs in the accounting system. The resulting percentage is the degree of accuracy the material cost data has in the CMMS. If the percentage is above 100%, then somehow the maintenance department is overbilling for spare parts. If the percentage is below 100%, then the maintenance department is not recording all of its spare part transactions and costs.

Strengths

This indicator is mandatory for any company striving to insure complete accuracy of its maintenance material charges.

Weaknesses

The weakness of this indicator is that sometimes it forces a maintenance organization to try to balance the numbers. At times, the organization may open standing or blanket work orders as a quick fix to try to cover the differences in the systems. This action should not be taken. The real issue is that somewhere the spare parts data is not being recorded against the appropriate equipment item. The errors should be traced, then corrected.

3. Percentage of Maintenance Contracting Costs Recorded in CMMS /EAM System

This indicator is similar to the previous two. It compares the maintenance contractor costs captured in the CMMS /EAM to the maintenance contractor costs captured in the accounting system. If the CMMS /EAM is part of or integrated to an Enterprise Resource Planning system, or even a general ledger system, then the reconciliation is not optional; the costs must match. This indicator insures that all contractor costs are recorded correctly. Many organizations are not effective in recording contractor costs to specific equipment items. This area is one of concern, especially if a company uses a high proportion of outside contractors. In some companies, contractors are paid from a different account, and the maintenance department never sees the actual costs. This issue may need attention in many companies.

Total Maintenance Contracting Costs in CMMS/EAM*
Total Maintenance Contracting Costs from Accounting

This indicator is derived by dividing the maintenance contractor costs recorded in the CMMS (and EAM) by the maintenance contractor costs in the accounting system. The resulting percentage is the degree of accuracy the contractor cost data has in the CMMS/EAM. If the percentage is above 100%, then somehow the contractor costs are excessive. If the percentage is below 100%, then the maintenance department is not recording all of the contractor costs.

Strengths

This indicator is mandatory for any company striving to insure complete accuracy of its maintenance contractor charges.

Weaknesses

The weakness of this indicator is that sometimes it forces a maintenance organization to try to balance the numbers. At times, the organization may open standing or blanket work orders as a quick fix to try to cover the differences in the systems. This action should not be taken. The real issue is that somewhere the contractor data is not being recorded against the appropriate equipment item. The errors should be traced and corrected.

A second major weakness is that not all CMMS/EAM systems accurately track contractor costs. In some systems it is a manual entry and must be manually posted. If a company utilizes many outside contract services, a CMMS/EAM that supports this function should be selected and implemented to insure accurate data collection.

4. Percentage of Equipment Coverage by CMMS/EAM System

This indicator examines how many of the equipment items in the plant are covered by the CMMS equipment history. During implementation of a CMMS, many companies take a short cut and enter only the critical equipment. This shortcut leaves second- and third-tier equipment without coverage in the CMMS. The costs against these levels of equipment are instead charged to a standing or blanket work order. However, the information is virtually unusable for data analysis, equipment troubleshooting, or life cycle costing. Eventually, all equipment, even if it is at a system level, must be entered into the CMMS.

$$\frac{\text{Total Number of Equipment Items in CMMS*}}{\text{Total Number of Equipment Items in the Plant}}$$

This indicator is derived by dividing the total number of equipment items entered into the CMMS by the total number of identified equipment items in the plant or facility. Although some equipment systems are broken down to the component level, others (especially non-critical units) can be left at the system level. This choice allows for data collection against the equipment item, without making the process too detailed. The alternative of not collecting any data is unacceptable.

Strengths

This indicator is mandatory for any company striving to insure complete accuracy of the maintenance data and being able to charge all costs and repair to the appropriate equipment history. It is a valuable tool for insuring complete equipment coverage.

Weaknesses

The weakness of this indicator is that sometimes it forces a maintenance organization to try to balance the numbers. At times, the organization may open standing or blanket work orders as a quick fix to try to cover the differences in the systems. This action should not be taken. The real issue is that the proper time and resources must be taken during the CMMS implementation. If the data in the CMMS is to be accurate, then all equipment items must be in the CMMS, even if non-critical items are at the system level.

5. Percentage of Stores Coverage by CMMS / EAM System

This indicator examines the extent to which inventory and spare parts in the plant are covered by the CMMS. During implementation of a CMMS, many companies take a shortcut and enter only critical or major spare parts into the CMMS. This leaves the majority of stores items (usually over 50%) without CMMS coverage. The costs for these spare parts are difficult to reconcile, so these items are charged to standing or blanket purchase order. The information is virtually unavailable for data analysis, equipment troubleshooting, or life cycle costing at the equipment level. Eventually all spare parts must be entered into the CMMS.

Total Number of Part Items in CMMS*
Total Number of Part Items in the Plant

This indicator is derived by dividing the total number of spare parts (also called stores line items) entered into the CMMS by the total number of identified spare parts in the plant or facility. Although this information may be difficult to derive, it is usually available from the procurement department.

Strengths

This indicator is mandatory for any company striving to insure complete accuracy of the inventory and procurement data, and being able to charge the parts cost to the appropriate equipment history. It is a valuable tool for insuring complete cost accuracy.

Weaknesses

The weakness of this indicator is that sometimes it forces a maintenance organization to try to fabricate information. In many cases, the organization doesn't know a part number or buys directly from vendors.

All too often, the information about the part, its cost, and the vendor is never recorded. These cases make accurate data tracking impossible. They also lengthen procurement times, because the next time the part is required, someone will have to look up all of the ordering information. Tracking all of the spare parts through the CMMS can help shorten the lead times for procurement.

6. Percentage of PM Coverage by CMMS / EAM System

This indicator examines the level of preventive maintenance coverage in the CMMS. By examining the total number of equipment items and comparing it to the average number of preventive maintenance tasks for an equipment item, a theoretical goal can be derived. By comparing the current number of preventive maintenance tasks to this number, one can approximate the level of coverage. A piece of equipment may have the following tasks interval:

- Daily

- Weekly

- Monthly

- Quarterly

- Semi-annual

- Annual

- Other

Few, if any, equipment items will have all of these intervals. But what if they each had on average three? Then the number of equipment items multiplied times three should be the theoretical number of preventive maintenance tasks for the plant or facility. In reality, most companies don't put this level of detail into their preventive maintenance programs.

Total Number of Preventive Maintenance Tasks*
Total Number of Equipment Items in the Plant X 3

This indicator is derived by dividing the total number of preventive maintenance tasks identified in the CMMS by the total number of equipment items in the CMMS multiplied by three. The goal is 100%. This indicator provides a theoretical check, but over 15 years of usage has shown it to provide an accurate check on preventive maintenance coverage in a CMMS.

Strengths

This indicator is essential for any company striving to insure that the preventive maintenance program completely covers the equipment entered into the CMMS.

Weaknesses

The weakness of this indicator is that it is just an average guideline. Even though time has proven it to be accurate, some companies will average fewer preventive maintenance tasks than 3 per equipment item. Others will average more. This indicator should never be used as a performance indicator, only as a suggested guideline.

7. Percentage of Maintenance Information Recorded at the Equipment Level

This indicator examines the amount of cost information that is recorded at the equipment level compared to untracked or unspecified cost information. This indicator is useful for discovering how much of the maintenance cost cannot be traced to a specific equipment item for data analysis, equipment troubleshooting, or life cycle costing.

<u>Total Maintenance Costs Charged to Individual Equipment Items*</u>
Total Maintenance Costs from Accounting

This indicator is derived by dividing the total maintenance costs charged against an individual equipment item by the total maintenance costs from accounting. The resulting percentage is the cost that is traceable to an equipment item. The other costs are most likely charged to a standing or blanket work order or else go unrecorded.

Strengths

This indicator is mandatory for any company striving to insure that maintenance costs have been accurately tracked. It is a valuable tool for insuring complete cost accuracy.

Weaknesses

The weakness of this indicator is that sometimes it forces a maintenance organization to try to fabricate information. The organization may charge costs to equipment that were not actually incurred on the equipment, trying to account for all the costs and make the indicator look good.

8. Supervisory or Coaching Staffing Ratios

This indicator monitors the span of control for a front-line maintenance supervisor. In a traditional organization, the proper ratio is 1 supervisor for every 8–12 maintenance technicians. Some organizations have tried to extend the ratio, but such efforts usually result in wasted labor productivity that incurs greater cost than the savings from eliminating a supervisory position.

$$\frac{\text{Number of Maintenance Employees or Full Time Equivalents}}{\text{Number of Supervisors or Coaches}}$$

This indicator is derived by dividing the total number of maintenance employees or full-time equivalents by the number of maintenance supervisors. The ratio should range from 8:1 to 12:1. Any ratio over 12 results in ineffective supervision. If the number is less than 8, there is not sufficient work to justify the supervisor. The exception to this occurs when the total number of maintenance employees is less than 8. Then, the maintenance supervisor may still be required.

Strengths

This indicator is mandatory for any company striving to insure proper supervisory levels for the maintenance organization.

Weaknesses

The weakness of this indicator is that organizations try to de-emphasize the span of control of the supervisors or coaches by hiding under the concept of empowerment. The typical organization using this excuse has little understanding of what the legal requirements under the National Labor Relations Act and OSHA regulations actually involve. If these requirements are clearly understood, many companies could save themselves OSHA fines and civil lawsuits.

9. Planner Ratios

This indicator is used to monitor the span of control for a maintenance planner. In a traditional organization, the proper ratio is 1 planner for every 15–20 maintenance technicians. Some organizations have tried to extend the ratio, but such efforts usually result in wasted labor productivity that incurs greater cost than the savings from eliminating a planner's position.

$$\frac{\text{Number of Maintenance Employees or Full Time Equivalents}}{\text{Number of Planners}}$$

This indicator is derived by dividing the total number of maintenance employees or full-time equivalents (in the case of operations involvement or team-based maintenance) by the number of maintenance planners. The ratio should range from 15:1 to 20:1. Any ratio over 20 results in ineffective planning. If the number is less than 15, there is not sufficient work to justify the planner full time. The exception to this is when the total number of maintenance employees range from 8–15. Then the maintenance planner may still be required.

Strengths
This indicator is mandatory for any company striving to insure proper levels of planning and scheduling for the maintenance organization.

Weaknesses
The weakness of this indicator is that organizations try to de-emphasize the span of control of the planners by hiding under the concept of empowerment. The typical organization using this excuse has little understanding of what impact planning has on labor productivity. In organizations without planners, the hands-on or wrench time is low. When the work is planned, the wrench time is higher. Imagine a NASCAR pit crew working effectively without planning. The pit stop would be in minutes, not seconds. Planners have the same impact on maintenance labor productivity and equipment uptime.

10. Percentage of Maintenance Support to Direct Maintenance Costs

This indicator is used to monitor the support personnel required for the maintenance hourly technicians. In a traditional organization, the proper ratio is 1 support person for every 3–5 hourly maintenance technicians. Some organizations have been able to extend the ratio by applying easy-to-use CMMS for data collection and analysis. However, a CMMS that is not easy to use and is keystroke intensive may actually lower the ratio.

Total Number of Maintenance Overhead Personnel
Total Hourly Maintenance Personnel

This indicator is derived by dividing the total number of maintenance overhead personnel by the number of hourly maintenance personnel. The ratio should range from 3:1 to 5:1. Any ratio over 5 results in ineffective staffing. For example, it is more economical to pay a maintenance clerk to enter information than it is to pay a maintenance technician $20 or more an hour to enter data. A company does not want to staff the overhead roles too heavily, but it is just as costly to staff the roles too lightly.

Strengths
This indicator is mandatory for any company striving to insure proper levels of support for the maintenance organization.

Weaknesses
The weakness of this indicator is that organizations try to de-emphasize the support for the organization by hiding under the concept of empowerment. The typical organization using this excuse has little understanding of what impact the overhead functions have on the accuracy of the equipment maintenance data. If an organization desires to be competitive by utilizing maintenance data, it will provide the correct level of maintenance overhead personnel.

CMMS/EAM System Problems

As highlighted earlier, the overall usage of the CMMS as a tool is poor by the majority of organizations. Couple this with the fact that about 50% of all CMMSs are deemed to have failed after less than two years of operation, and there are clearly issues that must be addressed for the CMMS to be an effective tool for most organizations. The eight most common reasons are explained next.

1. Lack of Maintenance Dedication

This problem develops when the maintenance organization lacks clear definition of their roles and responsibilities. The organization may actually believe that maintenance is a necessary evil, insurance, or just an overhead expense. Instead of focusing on value-added functions, it focuses on reactive maintenance. This type of maintenance organization needs education on what equipment management really entails. Unless it develops a proactive attitude by understanding the impact it can make on the company's profitability, it will never be dedicated to Best Practice maintenance concepts (including full usage of its CMMS) and will never improve.

2. Poor or Incomplete Implementation

This is a typical problem for organizations that never fully understood the implementation costs for a CMMS. The rule of thumb is that the software is somewhere between 1/3 and 1/5 of the total cost of the implementation. If the budget for the implementation is insufficient, then the data collection and training of the end users is often eliminated. The organization may believe the employees can figure out how to use the software: after all, the salesmen said it was easy to use. The organization also figures that the hourly technicians can gather the data as they work. This never happens. As a result, the CMMS is underutilized and the implementation fails; the return on investment in the CMMS is never realized.

3. Lack of End User Training on CMMS

Although this problem was partially covered before, it deserves special mention. No matter how easy a CMMS appears to be, never shortcut the end-user training. Microsoft Windows is supposed to be very easy to use, but how many casual users ever realize the power of the operating system? The same is true for any CMMS. Unless the end users are trained, the full power of the system is never realized. Lack of training is the single biggest factor in the overall failure of the CMMS as a maintenance tool.

4. Lack of Sufficient Resources

If a company is to utilize a CMMS successfully, it must remember that "Someone must feed the monster." The system requires certain amounts of data to be entered every day if it is to be effective. Unless the support resources are in place to insure data entry, the data is not input. Without the data being entered in a timely fashion, the CMMS has nothing of value with which to manage maintenance. The labor resources to operate the CMMS properly must be clearly defined during implementation and then be provided on an ongoing basis to insure there is value added in the data being provided by using the CMMS. Otherwise, another failure results.

5. Inaccurate Data in the CMMS

This problem is typically caused by partial or casual use of the CMMS. If there is no dedication to entering accurate data, the expression garbage in means garbage out finds fulfillment. The expression No data is better than bad data is also applicable. If any decisions are made based on the data in the CMMS, they are wrong, and the maintenance department loses credibility. In most cases, the rest of the organization knows the information in the maintenance system is inaccurate. Therefore, it is never allowed to be used to influence decisions and the CMMS is ruled a failure. Unless the resources and disciplines are in place to insure accurate data collection and usage, the CMMS will fail.

6. Not Utilizing the Data in the CMMS

This problem is a trap organizations fall into when they lose focus of the real value of the CMMS: to manage maintenance and the organization's equipment. The maintenance organization may have collected accurate data, but never have the time or the resources to analyze it. Therefore, it is collected, but never used. Eventually, the CMMS falls into a lack of use because no one ever sees any value from collecting the data. The only way to eliminate this problem is to plan from the beginning to use a maintenance or reliability engineer to analyze the data that will be collected. Without this focus, the CMMS will eventually fail.

7. Poorly Configured CMMS

This problem is a software issue. The vendor did not design the CMMS correctly and the system is difficult to configure. The modules may not cleanly integrate data between the work order and the stores or labor module. As a result, additional clerical support will be required. Because this increase wasn't planned, it is not in the budget and is usually not provided. In turn, the CMMS will fail. Before any CMMS is purchased (or built in-house, although no competitive organization really does this any more because they don't have the time, money, or resources), the end users should be consulted on what they want the CMMS to do for them and how it should do it. Therefore, functionality should be approved before it is ever purchased. If not, another failure will result.

8. Poor Buy-In by the Organization

This is similar to the first problem, except the rejection is organizational, not just by the maintenance department. In some cases, the CMMS is viewed as something that only the maintenance department uses, not as an organizational tool for managing the company's equipment. In other cultures, the CMMS is viewed as an Equipment Management Information System (EMIS). This reinforces the idea that it is not just a maintenance tool, but also an organizational tool. Unless the organization can see the value of the CMMS, it will not receive the acceptance it requires to be useful. This problem is overcome by the organization being educated to the value of good maintenance and data collection.

APPENDIX A

SAMPLE DETAILED MODULE
REQUIREMENTS SPECIFICATION

Equipment Subsystem

Overview

The system must include the ability to maintain a reference file of information on equipment, buildings, vehicles and other maintained items. In addition to static reference data, the equipment/facility catalog should also collect dynamic information related to the maintained item such as preventive, corrective and predictive maintenance information as well complete cost histories.

Minimum Capabilities

The equipment/facility catalog must include the following information: equipment/facility ID number, equipment/facility description, location information, assigned cost center, manufacturer, model number, manufacturer serial number, and equipment priority. **Vendors without existing software systems that meet these requirements should not respond to this section.**

3 Standard Feature	**2** Available in Next Release	**1** Available through Customization	**0** Not Available

Function	Response	Comment/Ref.

1. General Requirements

    A. Users must be able to locate equipment/facility records without knowing the equipment/facility ID number. The following search criteria should be supported:

        (1) Parent ID number

        (2) Keyword description (e.g. "lathe" or "building") and associated qualifiers (e.g. "turret" or "no. 4")

            a. "Sounds like" query

            b. Wild card searches (starts with etc.)

        (3) Equipment/facility type
            (e.g. "digester" or "academic")

        (4) Stock number

        (5) Cost center

        (6) Area code or building number

        (7) WO number

    B. After the initial search has been conducted, the user should be able to sort the database by three auxiliary qualifiers:

        Example:

Keyword	Crane
Qualifier	Overhead
Aux. Qualifier 1	Span
Aux. Qualifier 2	Hoist
Aux. Qualifier 3	Production Line

        (1)   Sort by auxiliary qualifier

        (2)   Right or left justify (user-defined display options)

    C. The system should support a two-tiered inquiry. That is, after the user tells the system they want to look at all air handlers, they should have the option then say they want to look at all air handlers in Smith Hall.

    D. Allow the user to add fields of information

(1)   Establish field format (date, decimal etc.)

(2)   Copy templates (list of fields) to multiple maintained items

(3)   Copy field values (completed templates) to multiple items

(4)   Provide access to this information independent of the catalog so users can review it without being allowed to make changes to other areas of the history record.

E. Provide integrated access to an imaging system

(1)   Automatically transport equipment number

(2)   Return where you left off when completed

2. On-line Reference Information

A. Keyword description (UDT)

B. Qualifiers to further define keywords

C. Ability to change keyword/qualifier combinations and have those changes retroactively applied to existing equipment

D. At least three auxiliary descriptions to further describe the maintained item (e.g. "main hoist = 150 tons; span = 25 feet")

E. Accounting/purchasing information

(1)   Purchase contract, date and price, miles/hrs @ purchase

(2)   PO number, capital ID number, tax exempt flag (Y/N)

(3)   Miles/hrs @ sale, date sold, selling price

F. Subassemblies and parent ID

G. Location information

(1)   Area code or building/floor/room

(2)   Free form location description

H. Equipment/facility type (UDT) and inspection type (UDT)

I. Criticality factors

(1)   Equipment priority code (UDT)

a. Priority code and short description

        b. Detailed description

    (2)   Equipment status code (UDT)

        a. Status code, description

        b. Equipment priority code incorporated in WO priority calculation

    (3)   Out of service information

        a. From date

        b. To date

    (4)   Shutdown code (UDT)

        To be used in WO system and other areas to indicate the shutdown status of the equipment.

        a. Normal operation

        b. Unscheduled shutdown

        c. Extended shutdown

        d. Power reduction

J. Automatic PM notice print flag (Y/N)

    If set to yes, the system should generate a notice each time a PM is issued. This notice can then act as a reminder to other plant personnel that a PM will be conducted in their area on a specific date.

K. Drawing number, last revision date

L. The equipment/building number format must be user-defined

3. Equipment/Facility Cross-Referencing/Analysis

A. Sub-assembly management

    (1)   Track up to 999 subassemblies

    (2)   Allow system transactions (charging labor, issuing material etc.) to be charged to a subassembly

        a. Accumulate to the assembly "cost bucket"

        b. Simultaneously accumulate to the assigned

equipment item's "cost bucket"

(3) Maintain on-line reference of subassemblies for each equipment item

(4) Allow parts to be assigned at the subassembly level for the purposes of building a BOM

B. Parent-child management
In addition to subdividing a maintained item into subassemblies, the system should be able to associate equipment items into a system for historical analysis. This is particularly important when maintaining large complex systems like a building HVAC system which may include dozens of pieces of equipment (compressors, air handling units, vents etc.) For this reason, each maintained item should be able to be referenced to a "Parent" maintained item for historical analysis.

(1) One parent per maintained item

(2) Unlimited hierarchy of parent-child relationships

(3) Automatic roll-up of all maintenance/repair costs

(4) On-line navigation from parent to child and other

related maintained items

4. On-line Access to WOs

A. Access to full schedule of PM program including:

(1) Crew and craft assigned to do task

(2) Base date when PM started, PM frequency

(3) Next date PM is scheduled/last time performed

(4) Number of times PM performed year-to-date

(5) List dates (if PM is scheduled for specific dates)
B. Corrective maintenance (CM)

(1) Query WO backlog by:

a. Open WOs

b. Closed WOs

c. Both open and closed WOs

(2) Enter secondary selection criteria:

   a. WO description

   b. Subassembly code

   c. WO originators

   d. WO types

   e. Failure codes

   f. Reconciliation codes

   g. Project numbers

   h. Reference number (user-defined)

   i. Shutdown codes

   j. WO status code

   k. Shutdown code

   l. Equipment priority code

   m. WO priority code

   n. Stock numbers

   o. Date range of WO (entry date)

   p. Date range of WO (close date)

   q. Ability to enter multiple secondary values
     (project numbers "123, 345, 567")

   r. Ability to enter multiple criteria
     (stock no. "#123" and failure code "seized shaft")

(3) Provide access to the individual WO detail including:

   a. General/header information, cost detail

   b. Text/instructions, WO notes

   c. Tools and material used/required

5. **On-line Cost Information The system must display on-line detail and summary costs and statistics for each maintained item.**

A. PM data including:

(1) Last overhaul date and last overhaul WO number

(2) Last meter reading and reading date

B. Down time information (hours)

(1) Period to date, year to date and life to date

(2) Rolling summary of past twelve months

C. Maintenance cost/statistics history

(1) Primary selection criteria

a. Category/subassembly

b. Work type

c. Electrical work, mechanical work or both

d. For primary item, equipment subs or both

e. Total

(2) Displays on-line:

a. Cost data

i. Labor cost

ii. Direct material cost

iii. Warehouse material cost

iv. Service cost

v. Total cost

b. Statistics

i. Number of WOs

ii. Labor hours

c. Display information in tabular format by:

        i. Period-to-date

        ii. Year-to-date

        iii. Last year

        iv. Previous year 2

        v. Previous year 3

        vi. Previous year 4

        vii. Previous year 5

        viii. Lifetime-to-date

(3) All costs and statistics automatically updated from other transactions in the system.

6. Predictive Maintenance System

A. Maintain inspection reading limits for each item

B. Track and record:

(1) Form of measurements (e.g.: degrees Fahrenheit, Hz)

(2) Base reading

(3) Highest acceptable reading

(4) Lowest acceptable reading

(5) User-defined test points

(6) Historical data maintained on-line for trend analysis

C. Readings entered via WO or through a stand-alone program

D. Integrate equipment meter reading with WOs so PMs are automatically generated based on equipment reading

E. Export information through a macro for spreadsheet plotting

F. Allow integration to predictive maintenance monitoring systems (infrared sensing, vibration analysis etc.)

7. Free-form Notes

A. Unlimited free-form notes for each maintained item

B. Automatically record and display author

C. Display notes by date (most recent displayed first)

D. Display subject heading with unlimited text behind summary
E. Allow the user to identify word processing conventions

F. Provide access to notes independent of the catalog so users can read equipment notes without being allowed to make changes to other areas of the catalog

G. Options to add, change, delete and print notes

8. Equipment Bill of Material (BOM)
   A. Ability to inquire on the parts list to create BOM

   B. Copy one BOM to another equipment item

   C. Allow parts lists to be built for equipment items or subassemblies

   D. Support multilevel parts lists (parts lists within parts lists)

   E. Allow stock or direct items to be added to the BOM

   F. Prevent duplicate parts from being added to the same BOM

   G. If the user tries to add an item with an existing mfgr. part number, the system should display those stock items with the entered mfgr. part number. After reviewing the list, the user should have the option to add the part to the BOM.

   H. On-line equipment BOM displays:

      (1) Stock number/description

      (2) Manufacturer part number, keyword description of part

      (3) Part or assembly flag (P/A)

      (4) Quantity and unit of measure

   I. Allow stock system inquiry from BOM

   J. "Reverse BOM" displays equipment items on which a part is installed

      (1) Use part number to perform query

      (2) Allow the user to query the database without knowing the part ID (use keyword description of part, manufacturer's part number etc.)

   (3) Display:

     a. Stock number, description

     b. Row/bin, quantity-on-hand (QOH)

     e. For each equipment the part is installed on:

       i. Equipment and category number

       ii. Description and quantity installed

9. Building File Maintenance

The system must support the maintenance of an on-line building file. This file should be in the form of a user defined table and should be accessible whenever the system requests for a "Building Number." The building file should maintain the following information:

A. Building number (user-defined format)

B. Short building name (used in displays and searches)

C. Full building name, number of floors

D. 3 lines of address

E. Free-form notes and comments

F. Room Information

   (1) Number of rooms

   (2) Room number (user-defined format)

   (3) Room description

G. Default chargeback account numbers including % distributions

10. Standard System Reports
   A. Period equipment cost report by work type

   B. Period equipment cost report by cost center

   C. Period equipment cost report by equipment number

   D. Parts list print

   E. BOM adjustment report
   This report should list all stock issues in which the item issued was not on the equipment BOM.

APPENDIX B
THE PAST AND THE FUTURE

Are We There Yet?

The words, "Are we there yet?" are among the most-feared words parents can hear on a long trip with their offspring. What the kids are asking, in a simpler form, is, "Haven't we been doing this long enough to have arrived?" As PEM magazine celebrates its 30th Anniversary, we are over a quarter of a century into our journey toward maintenance and engineering excellence, and it seems appropriate to ask the same question: Are we there yet?

The Way It Was

Thirty years ago, what was the status of the maintenance and engineering functions?

In many companies, they were overhead functions, thought of as necessary evils. In the mid-70s, it was difficult to determine if the maintenance and engineering functions were kept around as insurance or were really valuable parts of organizations.

Most organizations had traditional hierarchical structures. They were managed by command-and-control-type managers who learned their management skills from the military. The tools used then were not nearly as technically advanced as those available today. In fact, there were few computer control systems, and PLCs were just being accepted into plants. There were few proactive maintenance techniques in use, although focused planning and scheduling were becoming common.

At that time, computerized maintenance management systems were unknown. There simply were no CMMSs. Any maintenance records that were kept were in file cabinets, and there was little, if any, analysis of the data in those cabinets. Data accuracy and integrity were not a priority.

Because many of the craftspeople were trained in the military during military conflicts of the past decades, the work force of 25 years ago had relatively good skills. However, cross training was not an option. Everyone specialized in his or her own craft.

Technology was evolving and some predictive maintenance (PDM) tools

217

were beginning to develop. However, they were just islands of technology, with the results not being fed into the overall maintenance strategy. Rather, the PDM technicians would take their readings and verbally pass on their observations, which were rarely acted upon.

Technical initiatives, such as Reliability Centered Maintenance (RCM) was just getting started. The original studies were conducted in the early 1960s and were quickly accepted by the airline and the nuclear energy industry. The Total Productive Maintenance (TPM) techniques were gaining acceptance and they were being spread abroad. The proliferation of TPM was accelerated by the publication and translation of dozens of Japanese textbooks on the topic.

Where Are We Now?

What is the situation today, 30 years into our trip?

In some companies, maintenance and engineering are seen as value added—or, perhaps better, as value adding—functions. However, in most companies, they are still viewed as reactive and an overhead expense.

Organizational structures have changed, moving from hierarchical structures to decentralized business units or, in some companies, functional teams. Unfortunately, many companies have lost their focus on their technical capabilities and have actually downsized much of the technical expertise out of their organizations. As a result, the organization's maintenance and reliability initiatives have been left floundering. Wanting to show progress, they have focused their efforts on soft skills programs, which have showed minimal, if any, return on investment. In many of these cases, maintenance and reliability quickly loses their standing in the organization and becomes a costly overhead function.

Unfortunately, most of the advanced maintenance strategies have not provided the benefits that were forecast. Despite their benefits, only a small number of companies have utilized advanced strategies such as RCM and TPM in their maintenance and reliability organizations. It seems that there are pockets of excellence in the industries, but there is no large wave of companies successfully adopting advanced maintenance strategies. Many are still struggling to succeed with their preventive maintenance or MRO inventory and purchasing processes.

Today's PDM tools are, of course, more technically advanced. Companies use predictive technologies to monitor and trend equipment conditions in order to make repair-or-replace decisions before failure. This approach, coupled with a reliability philosophy, has done much to increase equipment utilization and preparedness. In reality, however, most of the PDM programs are underutilized, still not fully integrated into the maintenance and reliability strategy for the company's equipment and assets.

CMMSs have advanced from computerized file cabinets to useful tools for managing maintenance and reliability functions. Today, equipment data is tracked and trended with a focus on achieving lower life-cycle costs. In many cases, the trend is to use a CMMS that is part of an overall company system. With this extended utilization, the CMMS evolves into an enterprise wide system, commonly referred to as an Enterprise Asset Management System (EAM).

The general skill level of the work force, by contrast, has declined. The highly-skilled craftspeople have retired, only to be replaced by those who have not received adequate training in apprenticeships. In fact, many apprenticeship programs have been discontinued or diluted. Although technology has increased in the plants and facilities, a supporting focus on technical training has not developed. This situation represents a major detour on the journey to maintenance excellence.

What Lies Ahead?

What does the map show for the next part of our trip?

With companies being pressured by owners and shareholders to deliver higher levels of financial performance, the maintenance and reliability functions will finally be moved into the limelight. Corporate executives will realize the financial benefit properly organized, staffed, and trained maintenance and reliability organization can deliver. With this breakthrough understanding, advancements in maintenance and reliability will accelerate.

Organizational structures will be modified to fit a holistic understanding of maintenance and reliability. The focus must be on staffing with skilled personnel who can help ensure equipment and asset performance. The reduction of redundant organizational functions and the resultant high costs will be replaced with a more centralized approach, using the maintenance and reliability functions as optimizers of equipment effectiveness. This focus will give the maintenance and reliability organizations higher visibility in the overall corporate structure, leading to positions such as the Corporate Maintenance and Reliability Officer (CMRO, CMO, or CRO).

The technology tools will continue to evolve, including the development of self-diagnostics and artificial intelligence for equipment troubleshooting and problem solving. The maintenance techniques of today—RCM, TPM, PDM, CMMS, etc.—will evolve into a holistic approach that integrates the required techniques to maximize equipment effectiveness and return on net assets (RONA).

CMMSs will all be replaced by EAM (Enterprise Asset Management) systems. The features will include real-time monitoring and on-line diagnostics for immediate answers to developing problems. These advances, too, will help organizations optimize their returns on their assets.

Successful organizations will re-focus the skills of their work forces to include a detailed understanding of the operating dynamics of the equipment. Where this happens, the meaning of "craft" will be returned to maintenance, as each individual craftsperson becomes a maintenance professional. As technologies develop and are implemented in plants, the skills needed to maintain the technology as well as the equipment will become increasingly important.

So, are we there yet? Well, we are on our way; but we are not there yet. The trip has been interesting so far and promises to be even more interesting and challenging during the next 30 years. The question we have to ask is "Are YOU ready to face the challenges awaiting maintenance and reliability professionals in the future?"

Who Will Feed the Monster?

In the effort to improve their maintenance organizations, many companies have purchased computerized maintenance management systems (CMMS / EAM systems). In most organizations, the purchase of a CMMS / EAM system is an exciting time. There is new hardware, new software, new training, and opportunities to interface with the system vendor's personnel. But soon, the "new" times are over. Soon the CMMS / EAM System owner discovers the system can't be used until someone feeds the databases. This means someone must load the following information into the system:

- Equipment numbering schemes
- Equipment nameplate information
- Spare parts numbering schemes
- Spare parts nameplate information
- Preventive maintenance procedures
- Vendor identification information.

If, for example, a company has 2000 pieces of equipment, 3000 items in stores, about 3000 regular preventive maintenance tasks (PMs), and 150 vendors, and it takes one hour per item to gather and load this information, then it will take four employees about three months to feed the databases. And that must occur before the company can properly use the system.

Three months later...

Now the company feels it is ready to use the CMMS / EAM system. It will be beneficial to track work orders, keep track of labor and materials, and provide the historical data necessary for the maintenance manager to make good decisions and track indicators (mean time between failures and mean time to repair, for example). This is what the manager has been waiting to do—manage maintenance. So, the maintenance manager tries to run a report and see, for example, the equipment history for Pump #586. But wait a minute. It's blank. What's wrong? They call the CMMS / EAM system vendor and complain that there's a problem.

The vendor asks if they have been entering work orders, the related costs, and posting the information to the equipment history. The company employees reply, "Do we have to do all that work?" The vendor points out that in order to effectively use its CMMS / EAM system the company must daily:

- Enter work orders
- Add all employees' time, all material used, all contractor costs, and any equipment rental costs to the work orders
- Close the work orders to history
- Plan any new work orders that have been requested
- Enter and close any emergency work orders for the day
- Reorder any spare parts below the minimum stock quantities
- Generate any meter PMs that are due
- Generate the necessary daily reports

In addition, weekly, the company must:

- Develop, approve, and finalize the weekly schedule
- Generate any calendar PMs that are due
- Generate the scheduled work orders
- Generate store pick tickets for the work orders on the schedule
- Generate any necessary weekly reports

The maintenance manager says, "But I don't have enough people to do all of that work. No one told me I would have to provide staff to do this." The vendor says, "Well, I am sorry, but somebody has to feed the monster." At the time of purchase, the buyer overlooked or ignored the effort and cost associated with feeding the "hungry monster."

Unfortunately, this scenario plays out in too many companies today. CMMS / EAM system vendors have a responsibility to tell customers about the staff time required to keep CMMS / EAM systems fed. But too often buyers consider only the purchase price. When that happens, the CMMS / EAM system does not get used effectively and the projected savings and benefits used to justify its purchase fail to materialize. Unless more companies consider the ongoing resource requirements, we will continue to see systems under-optimized. If you are purchasing a CMMS / EAM system, don't fail to count the cost of feeding and, thereby, taming the monster.

Downsizing or Dumbsizing: Which?

For every action there is an equal and opposite reaction.
-Sir Isaac Newton

Companies today are using terms such as rightsizing, downsizing, and re-engineering to describe the process of reducing the size or changing the strategic direction of their organizations. Many of these decisions to change are made without consulting the personnel who must implement the changes or live with the results. In many cases, upper management requires plant managers, supervisors, and line personnel to do more tasks with fewer resources. Deciding to change an organization, without consulting those affected, increases the probability that the decision is the wrong one.

Consider, for example, the plant and facilities engineering and maintenance groups. Engineering and maintenance within an organization are technical disciplines. So, decisions affecting engineering and maintenance should be made by decision makers with technical backgrounds. However, in most companies, decisions are not made by those most qualified to make them.

For example, there is the classic case of reducing the number of operations personnel by a certain percentage. Then, all support functions find out they must reduce by the same percentage. Now, does reducing the number of operations personnel reduce the engineering and maintenance workload? No, because the engineering and maintenance workload relates to the facility's assets and equipment. Unless the facility sells off some of its assets or equipment, the engineering and maintenance workload does not change. But the reductions are made anyway because non-technical managers don't understand these facts.

So, what happens? The engineering and maintenance organizations still try to do their jobs, but little things—the maintenance and engineering basics—fall by the wayside as maintenance and engineering personnel scramble to react to situations. With time, the little things continue to build until they become big problems. This leads to additional reactive activities, which in turn lead to more neglect of maintenance and engineering basics. The situation continues as a downward spiral until the organization is out of control. Equipment downtime continues to increase and deterioration of the equipment's condition also continues. Maintenance record keeping and organizational effectiveness also suffer, because the resources needed to record events are not available.

Finally, the company no longer is able to effectively produce its product or provide its service because the physical plant and equipment have deteriorated. In the absence of accurate engineering and maintenance data, decisions about the repair or replacement of equipment are based solely on opinions. This leads to increased capital equipment expenditures as the company replaces prematurely deteriorating equipment. It also may lead to unnecessary investment in excess capacity in order to compensate for poor maintenance and engineering practices. The company eventually cannot stay in business.

Was this rightsizing, downsizing, or re-engineering? No, it was just bad decision making by company officials unqualified to make these decisions. Smartsizing vs. stupidsizing: that's each company's choice. Let's just hope more companies make the right choice.

The Challenge of Change

In the movie *The American President,* the fictitious president holds a press conference at the end of the movie to defend himself against his main competitor for re-election. In concluding, he says that his opponent is interested in only two things:

1. Making people afraid of their problems
2. Telling them who is to blame for their problems

In examining the changing role of maintenance management in companies today, perhaps something could be learned from these quotes.

Companies today are facing ever-increasing competitive pressures, which are forcing them to streamline their business processes to eliminate waste. In addition, companies are implementing new methodologies that can establish and increase their competitive advantages. There have been some successes generated by these efforts. However, some companies have failed in these initiatives by perverting re-engineering efforts into downsizing, producing personnel layoffs, and decimating the technical resources in their organization.

Does this mean we should fear change? Should we stop looking for newer, more competitive methodologies? Some would have us be afraid of these initiatives and blame the results on executive management or the accountants. Some would have us not try to change our processes, feeling that the way we have always done things is good enough, then blame visionaries (who may be slightly ahead of their times) for the problems that have resulted.

Comparisons

What can be learned from some other initiatives, such as Theory of Constraints, Total Quality, or Lean Manufacturing? These initiatives, when implemented correctly, eliminated waste and improved a company's competitive position.

What is similar in maintenance management? Foundation initiatives such as planning and scheduling have eliminated waste, thus saving money. Also, advanced initiatives like Reliability Centered Maintenance (RCM) and Total Productive Maintenance (TPM), when implemented correctly, have increased company's efficiency and effectiveness, thus making them more competitive.

There are those who will downplay these strategic initiatives and say the majority are not really successful. However, one would do well to examine other World Class initiatives—tor example, the Malcolm Baldridge Award, the Quality Cup, or even ISO-9000 (or 14000) certifications. Of the hundreds of thousands of organizations in North America, how many have competed for these awards? Or even more striking, how many have won these awards? Does this mean that companies shouldn't even consider applying or trying to qualify for these awards? Are they a waste of time?

One would only have to read the case studies of companies that have won the awards or competed for the awards to answer the questions. The companies will confess that they learned so much from the competition. They learned about themselves and other companies and, in the educational process, made changes and became more competitive. The more they changed, the easier change became.

What about maintenance management or asset management? Again one could look at the NAME award, the "Best of the Best" designation, or even the

FAME award. Only a minority of companies ever really qualify or compete for these awards. But what are the results? Again, they make improvements based on what they learn about their companies and companies they study. These companies are utilizing tools and techniques like RCM, TPM, or self managed workforces. Yes, the majority of companies are not seeing huge benefits from these initiatives. But is that because the initiative is flawed or is it the company's implementation of the initiative that is flawed?

In *The American President,* the fictitious president also says that "you gather a group of middle aged, middle class citizens who remember with longing a better way of life, and then you tell them who is to blame for their problems." This could be true of mid-level managers and even line employees in many companies today. There have been many changes that blur lines of responsibilities, such as team-based organizations, or self-directed workforces. These initiatives will create confusion and conflict and a lack of clear direction for many companies. Does this mean the initiatives changes are bad? No, for there are companies achieving tremendous benefits from self-directed workforces and team-based activities.

The reality is that many World Class initiatives are not widely successful for quite common reasons:

- TPM: Fails due to a lack of education of what TPM really is and the resources to properly implement and sustain it.

- RCM: Fails due to a lack of education of RCM methodologies and the resources to properly sustain it.
- Self-Directed Workforces / Team-Based Organizations: Fail due to a lack of training for the workforce and management truly enabling the workforce by providing the necessary business information for the workforce to make financial based decisions.

So if someone says "these new initiative have no value," is it that they are trying to make you afraid of your problems and keep doing business as usual? Do they blame executive management for making wrong decisions, creating a rift between different organizations in the company? Is it really true that executive management or the accountants don't want the company to be successful? That they want it to fail? Or is it something else?

In *The American President,* it was said that people will listen to anyone who has center stage, simply because they are not educated enough to know if the person is right or wrong. Is that the case with maintenance or asset management? Isn't the real problem with many strategic initiatives that it sounds good, but people don't really understand if it is or not? Isn't it the case that as a society Americans want instant gratification? We don't give some of the initiatives enough time or resources before we pronounce them a failure and move on to something else. This is commonly called the program of the month or the flavor of the month.

In reality, it is the lack of education about the impact of assets, their cost, the technical resources, and their impact on a company's financials that creates many of the problems that we see in maintenance management today. Company's fail to understand the technical resources required to design, manufacture, install, operate, and maintain assets. This lack of vision prevents companies from ever establishing a life-cycle philosophy and optimizing their investment in their assets.

The only real solution is to establish a financial-based understanding of equipment technologies so that all organizations in the entire company are held accountable for the financial impact of their decisions. Although this will require time and effort to educate the company in this manner, it is the only true solution to improving the success rate of maintenance and asset management initiatives.

The American President concludes with the comment that America is advanced citizenship, that you really have to want it. This is also true of being the best. There are sacrifices that will be made, challenges to be met, and obstacles to be overcome. There must be new and innovative thinking about assets and their cost impact on a company's profitability. When this is accomplished, there will be new challenges and more changes. It is all part of a continuous improvement culture. It is a way of life. Innovate or Evaporate — the choice is yours.

APPENDIX C
FINANCIAL CASE STUDIES

Equipment Efficiency Case Studies

1. Disk Drives

This case study looks at a manufacturing operation for disk drives. During the process, a robotic arm picks up a computer hard drive and repositions it for transfer to the next operation. A problem developed where the robotic arm was dropping the disk drives periodically. The operators were becoming frustrated and wanted management to replace the robot. A team was assembled and given the task of improving the robot's operation. They learned that the robot was dropping a disk on the average of one every half hour of operation. When the robot dropped the drive, the operator needed an average of five minutes to reposition and re-index the robot. The operators were asked what would be an acceptable level of performance. After conferring, they replied that they could accept the robot dropping a drive once every two hours.

Let's examine their answer. A dropped drive once every 2 hours in a 24-hour-a-day/7-day-a-week operation adds up to a considerable amount of time. The operators worked a 12-hour shift. One dropped drive every 2 hours at 5 minutes downtime per drop equals 30 minutes downtime per shift. Multiplying this amount times the 14 shifts the robot operates equals 7 hours of downtime per week. In turn, 7 hours of downtime times $10,000 per hour of production output is $70,000 of downtime every week. Finally, multiplying this number times the 50 weeks a year the plant operates leads to an amount of $3,500,000 worth of downtime —and this is the amount the team said it was willing to tolerate! The problem with the robot was ultimately resolved and has reduced the downtime to almost zero.

This example highlights a problem. If there was one single occurrence of seven hours of downtime during a week of operation, everyone would focus on finding and fixing the problem. However, if you divide the seven hours of downtime into five-minute increments and distribute them throughout the week, people tend to ignore them, believing that this is the way the equipment is supposed to operate. Numerous studies have shown that these small losses add up over time, causing more of a loss than do the large breakdowns. Unfortunately most people ignore these small losses. Using the overall equipment effectiveness calculation correctly can expose these small losses.

2. Water Softeners

This second case about equipment efficiencies looks at a water softener. A series of large water softeners were used to produce soft water that was turned into steam, then injected down a hole in an oil production facility to force out the crude oil for processing. In this study, the water softeners were the bottleneck, restricting the amount of steam that could be produced and, in turn, the amount of crude oil that could be extracted.

Because the water softeners were the problem, management requested capital funding for the purchase of a sixth water softener to increase the volume. While the purchase was being processed, the field personnel put a cross-functional team together to examine the water softener problem. As they examined the OEE of the softeners, they discovered that the performance efficiency was very low (mid 50s). Examining the losses, the team found that the operators were rejuvenating the softeners on different frequencies and using different procedures to perform the rejuvenation. These procedures impacted the quantity and quality of the soft water the softeners could produce.

The team developed standard schedules and procedures, then trained the operators on these procedures. Immediately the volume of soft water increased to the point the water softeners were no longer the process bottleneck. The local management was able to return the capital appropriation for the purchase of the sixth softener because it was no longer required. The savings to the company totaled $750,000. As this example indicates, understanding the true design output of equipment can help avoid overinvesting in assets. An important point to remember: expense dollars not expended become profit dollars.

Overall Equipment Effectiveness Case Studies
1. Plastic Injection Molding Press

This example looks at an automotive parts supplier to one of the major U.S. auto manufacturers. The supplier ran a plastic injection molding press that produced components on a schedule of three 8-hour shifts, 5 days per week (see Figure C-1). This schedule allowed for a total of 7200 minutes for possible production. The company had planned downtime of 600 minutes per week (20 minutes for lunch per shift plus two 10-minute breaks per shift), leaving a net available run time of 6600 minutes per week.

The total downtime losses averaged 4422 minutes per week, leaving an actual operating time of 2178 minutes. Availability was then calculated to be 33%. During the 2178 minutes that the equipment ran, it produced 14,986 pieces. With a design cycle time of .109 minutes per piece, the operational efficiency was 75%. On average, there were 600 rejects during the week; therefore, the rate of product quality was 96%. When availability (33%) was multiplied times the efficiency rate (75%) and quality rate (96%), the overall equipment effectiveness was only 24%.

Given that 85% is considered to be the goal for OEE, the supplier had a large opportunity for improvement. How do you convince peers and executives, however, that 24% is not good and we need to increase OEE by another 61 percentage points? Convincing senior managers to make decisions with only percentage points for data is a daunting task. A better solution would be to present the improvement plan based on financial incentives. It is necessary, therefore, to re-work the problem, inserting the numbers that would be necessary to achieve an 85% OEE. These calculations are shown in Figure C-2.

Figure C-1

Injection Molding Press

1.	Gross Time Available (8 X 60 = 480 min.)	7200 min.
2.	Planned Downtime (For PM, lunch, breaks,)	600 min.
3.	Net Available Run Time (Line 1 – Line 2)	6600 min.
4.	Downtime Losses (Breakdowns, Setups, Adjustments)	4422 min.
5.	Actual Operating Time (Line 3 – Line 4)	2718 min.
6.	Equipment Availability (Line 5/ Line3 X 100)	33%
7.	Total Output for Operating Time (Pieces, tons,)	14,986 pieces
8.	Design Cycle Time	109 min./piece
9.	Operational Efficiency (Line 8 X Line 7 / Line 5 X 100)	75%
10.	Rejects During Week	600 pieces
11.	Rate of Product Quality [(Line 7 – Line 10)/ Line 7 X100]	96%
12.	OEE (Line 6 X Line 9 X Line 11)	24%

Injection Molding Press

1.Gross Time Available	7200 min.
(8 X 60 = 480 min.)	
2.Planned Downtime	600 min.
(For PM, lunch, breaks,)	
3.Net Available Run Time	6600 min.
(Line 1 – Line 2)	
4.Downtime Losses	660 min.
(Breakdowns, Setups, Adjustments)	
5.Actual Operating Time	5940 min.
(Line 3 – Line 4)	
6.Equipment Availability	90%
(Line 5/ Line 3 X 100)	
7.Total Output for Operating Time	51,770 pieces
(Pieces, tons,)	
8.Design Cycle Time	109 min./piece
9.Operational Efficiency	95%
(Line 8 X Line 7 / Line 5 X 100)	
10.Rejects During Week	518 pieces
11.Rate of Product Quality	99%
[(Line 7 – Line 10) / Line 7 X100]	
12.OEE	85%
(Line 6 X Line 9 X Line 11)	

Figure C-2

The second example shows that in order to have 90% equipment availability, the downtime losses can not exceed 660 minutes. This improvement will increase the operating time to 90%. With the increased availability, the total output would increase to 51,770 pieces at a design cycle time of .109 minutes per piece. With these increased volumes, the quality rate increases to 99%, lowering the rejects to 518 pieces. The difference in production volumes between the 24% OEE and the 85% OEE is an increase of 36,784 pieces.

This improvement, although impressive, still needs to be taken a step further. Each piece has a selling price of $10.00. Multiplying the 36,784 pieces times $10.00 per piece yields a net difference in revenue of $367,840. This figure will get any executive's attention. Still, there is one additional step: to annualize the revenue differential. It amounts to an improvement of more than $19 million annually. With this kind of a business case, the focus becomes what a company would spend to increase revenue by $19 million annually. $1 million? $5 million?

This particular company had ten presses with an almost identical OEE. Now the revenue differential grows tenfold. Furthermore, the company was set to build a new facility next door to house additional presses needed because the current ones could not keep up with market demand.

Although this case study may seem unrealistic, it is true and representative of events that occur all too often in companies. Without a clear understanding of how OEE affects their asset base, many companies make poor decisions concerning their assets. Companies will continue to be competitive only if they clearly understand how their assets should be utilized to support their business goals and objectives.

2. Offshore Gas Compressors Case Study

This example is drawn from an oil and gas company. The compressors being studied were on a deep-water platform used to feed the gas output from the field into a pipeline to send it onshore. The problem with these particular compressors was that they were aging. Maintenance wanted to take them offline for a complete overhaul. Operations felt they could not afford the downtime and resulting lost production. The organization was at an impasse. After consulting with the area superintendent, it was decided to do a financial study. The cost of the overhaul and the resulting lost production would be weighed against the lost production caused by the decreased efficiency of the compressors.

Two compressors were on the platform. OEE results for each compressor are detailed in FigureC-3 and Figure C-4. The first compressor's results (Figure C-3) indicate that availability met the goal of greater than 90%. The operation efficiency, however, was only 62%, indicating lost efficiency due to internal wear of the compressor. Completing the calculation, we find that OEE was 57%.

Compressor

1. Gross Time Available	168 hours	
2. Planned Downtime	0 hours	
3. Net Available Run Time	168 hours	
(Line 1 − Line 2)		
4. Downtime Losses	13 hours	
(PM, breakdowns)		
5. Actual Operating Time	155 hours	
(Line 3 − Line 4)		
6. Equipment Availability	92%	
(Line 5/ Line 3 X 100%)		
7. Total Output for Operating Time	45.5 MCFM	
8. Design Output	73.5 MCFM	
9. Operational Efficiency	62%	
10. Rejected Product	0	
11. Rate of Product Quality	100%	
12. Overall Equipment Effectiveness	57%	

Figure C-3

The quality rate was not a factor in this particular example. Because the meter that was used to determine volume shipped was on the outlet of the compressor, there was no opportunity for rejects. If the gas went into the pipeline, the money was in the cash register. This particular example, therefore, has a two-part OEE instead of the traditional three-part OEE calculation.

The second compressor (Figure C-4) showed a lower availability, but had a higher operational efficiency. With quality again not a factor, OEE was 67%.

Now came the difficult part: establishing the business case. First, if the efficiency was improved, did they have the extra gas capacity to draw from in their well? The answer was yes because they had some wells restricted and others shut off. Therefore, additional capacity was available. Second, was the market sufficient to support the extra production? Again, the answer was yes because the company could sell whatever they could add to the pipeline without impacting the price of the gas.

The next step was to understand the gap between what the compressors were able to produce currently and what the output would be at 85% OEE. At the time, the weekly output from the two compressors was 150.5 MCFM, the output measurement of the gas. If the compressors were restored to 85% OEE level, the output would be 196.23 MCFM weekly, a difference of 45.73 MCFM per week.

This production volume then had to be converted into a financial

Compressor

1.	Gross Time Available	168 hours
2.	Planned Downtime	0 hours
3.	Net Available Run Time (Line 1 – Line 2)	168 hours
4.	Downtime Losses (PM, breakdowns)	25 hours
5.	Actual Operating Time (Line 3 – Line 4)	143 hours
6.	Equipment Availability (Line 5/ Line 3 X 100%)	85%
7.	Total Output for Operating Time	105 MCFM
8.	Design Output	133 MCFM
9.	Operational Efficiency	79%
10.	Rejected Product	0
11.	Rate of Product Quality	100%
12.	Overall Equipment Effectiveness	67%

Figure C-4

term. At the time of the study, the gas price was $2,290.00 per MCFM, a potential difference of $104,721.70 per week. Annualized, this amounted to almost $5.5 million.

Next, the cost of the overhaul had to be determined. First, the maintenance labor and materials to perform the overhaul were determined. Next, the lost production that would be incurred during the outage was calculated. The compressors would be overhauled one at a time to prevent the field from being shut down. The total estimated cost for the overhaul was $450,000.

Now, the return on investment can be estimated by comparing the cost of the overhaul, $450,000, to the projected additional throughput valued at approximately $5,445,500. In theory the payback period was approximately 30 days. Once these figures were presented to the superintendent, the decision was made to proceed with the overhaul. The superintendent had the finance department track the expenditures compared to the increased production after the overhaul. The payback was close to what was expected; the actual payback period was 28.1 days.

Consider the impact of converting the OEE to a dollar value. The maintenance department already tracked the efficiency of the compressors. The efficiency loss was already known prior to running the financial analysis. It was only when the loss was converted to dollars that a decision was made to move forward with the overhaul. Impasses between maintenance and operations can only be broken when the financial impact of the issue being debated is highlighted. Only then can the best decision for the company's profitability be derived.

3. Compressor Crankshaft Case Study

This case looks at a production line that makes crankshafts for a refrigerator compressor. The line was not able to make the target production rates, which were already lower than the design capacity of the line. The study revealed that the line was supposed to run 24 hours per day, 7 days per week. It was decided to look at this OEE on a monthly time frame, rather than by a shift, day, or week (see Figure 3-5).

Because OEE was monthly, a thirty-day window was examined. Thirty days times 24 hours per day produces 720 hours of availability. Availability should be 648 hours to achieve the goal of 90% availability.

Performance efficiency was not as easy to calculate. Maintenance, engineering, and production disagreed strongly about the actual design

Figure C-5

Crankshaft Line

A. Availability – Goal – 90%
   (30 days X 24 hours X .90)   648 Hours

B. Performance Efficiency
   A. (11,800/Day or 491.67/hour)   318,602 Parts
   B. (10,000/Day or 416/hour)   269,568 Parts
   C. (9,000/Day or 375/hour)   243,000 Parts

C. Quality Rate – Goal – 99% (99.99999%)
   A. =   315,415 Parts
   B. =   266,872 Parts
   C. =   240,570 Parts

production rate of the line. Almost everyone at the plant believed the production rate was 375 per hour. Researching documentation at the plant, older production reports indicated the line had at one time operated at 416 parts per hour. After contacting the vendor and other companies that had the same line, it was determined that the design production rate was 491.67 parts per hour. In order to reduce the amount of disagreement about the design production rate, it was decided to calculate OEE in a best case/likely case/worst case scenario. Figure C-5 shows how these calculations were made. The figures for both performance efficiency and quality rate show all three options.

The next step was to prepare the financial comparison. This step involved taking the production volumes for the past month and establishing the financial parameters. When the per-hour rates were projected for a 24-hour period and the best/likely/worst case production rates were compared, the results were calculated (see Figure C-6).

When the difference between what could have been made was compared to what was actually produced, the production differences were calculated. Each part had a shelf value of $16 and the production variances were multiplied times this amount to calculate the difference in dollars. The monthly variance ranged from a best case of $2,146,976 to a worst case of $949,440, as illustrated in Figure C-6.

The final step in the calculation is to annualize the potential savings, as shown in Figure C-7. The saving ranges from a best case of $25,763,712 to a worst case of $11,393,280. The question then asks what senior management would be willing to invest to see the increases in production and the subsequent financial return.

Crankshaft Line

Compared to the May Actuals (181,230)

A. 11,800 per day
315,415 – 181,230 = 134,185
X$16.00
$2,146,960.00

B. 10,000 per day
266,872 – 181,230 = 85,642
X$16.00
$1,370,272.00

C. 9,000 per day
240,570 – 181,230 = 59,340
X$16.00
$949,440.00

Figure C-6

Revenue Generation Annual Results

A. $2,146,900.00 X 12 mo. = $25,763,520.00

B. $1,370,272.00 X 12 mo. = $16,433,264.00

C. $949,440.00 X 12 mo. = $11,393,280.00

Figure C-7

In this case study, the final summary was presented to senior management. The numbers were not all that surprising to them. In fact, the Chief Financial Officer said he know of lines in other companies that ran at the best case production rates and thought the numbers that were presented were believable.

This company essentially had no formalized maintenance business process in place. Based on the return on investment presented, the senior management team decided to fund the improvement necessary to achieve the levels of production that were possible.

INDEX

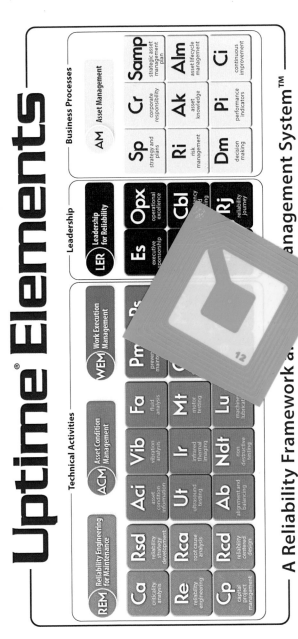

Uptime® Elements

A Reliability Framework and Asset Management System™

Reliabilityweb.com's Asset Management Timeline

Technical Activities

REM — Reliability Engineering for Maintenance

Ca — criticality analysis
Rsd — reliability strategy development
Re — reliability engineering
Rca — root cause analysis
Cp — capital project management
Rcd — reliability centered design

ACM — Asset Condition Management

Aci — asset condition information
Vib — vibration analysis
Fa — fluid analysis
Ut — ultrasound testing
Ir — infrared thermal imaging
Mt — motor testing
Ab — alignment and balancing
Ndt — non destructive testing
Lu — machine lubrication

WEM — Work Execution Management

Pm — preventive maintenance

Leadership

LER — Leadership for Reliability

Es — executive sponsorship
Opx — operational excellence
Cbl — competency based learning
Rj — reliability journey

Business Processes

AM — Asset Management

Sp — strategy and plans
Cr — corporate responsibility
Samp — strategic asset management plan
Ri — risk management
Ak — asset knowledge
Alm — asset lifecycle management
Dm — decision making
Pi — performance indicators
Ci — continuous improvement

Asset Lifecycle

Business Needs Analysis → Design → Create/Acquire → Operate / Maintain / Modify/Upgrade → Dispose/Renew → Residual Liabilities

reliabilityweb.com • maintenance.org • reliabilityleadership.com

Reliabilityweb.com® and Uptime® Magazine Mission: **To make the people we serve safer and more successful.** One way we support this mission is to suggest a reliability system for asset performance management as pictured above. Our use of the Uptime Elements is designed to assist you in categorizing and organizing your own Body of Knowledge (BoK) whether it be through training, articles, books or webinars. Our hope is to make YOU safer and more successful.

ABOUT RELIABILITYWEB.COM

Created in 1999, Reliabilityweb.com provides educational information and peer-to-peer networking opportunities that enable safe and effective reliability and asset management for organizations around the world.

ACTIVITIES INCLUDE:

Reliabilityweb.com® (www.reliabilityweb.com) includes educational articles, tips, video presentations, an industry event calendar and industry news. Updates are available through free email subscriptions and RSS feeds. **Confiabilidad.net** is a mirror site that is available in Spanish at www.confiabilidad.net.

Uptime® Magazine (www.uptimemagazine.com) is a bi-monthly magazine launched in 2005 that is highly prized by the reliability and asset management community. Editions are obtainable in both print and digital.

Reliability Leadership Institute® Conferences and Training Events (www.reliabilityleadership.com) offer events that range from unique, focused-training workshops and seminars to small focused conferences to large industry-wide events, including the International Maintenance Conference (IMC), MaximoWorld and The RELIABILITY Conference™ (TRC).

MRO-Zone Bookstore (www.mro-zone.com) is an online bookstore offering a reliability and asset management focused library of books, DVDs and CDs published by Reliabilityweb.com.

Association of Asset Management Professionals

(www.maintenance.org) is a member organization and online community that encourages professional development and certification and supports information exchange and learning with 50,000+ members worldwide.

A Word About Social Good

Reliabilityweb.com is mission-driven to deliver value and social good to the reliability and asset management communities. *Doing good work and making profit is not inconsistent,* and as a result of Reliabilityweb.com's mission-driven focus, financial stability and success has been the outcome. For over a decade, Reliabilityweb.com's positive contributions and commitment to the reliability and asset management communities have been unmatched.

Other Causes

Reliabilityweb.com has financially contributed to include industry associations, such as SMRP, AFE, STLE, ASME and ASTM, and community charities, including the Salvation Army, American Red Cross, Wounded Warrior Project, Paralyzed Veterans of America and the Autism Society of America. In addition, we are proud supporters of our U.S. Troops and first responders who protect our freedoms and way of life. That is only possible by being a for-profit company that pays taxes.

I hope you will get involved with and explore the many resources that are available to you through the Reliabilityweb.com network.

Warmest regards,
Terrence O'Hanlon
CEO, Reliabilityweb.com